BIBLICAL SNAKES, BIBLICAL LADDERS

Biblical Snakes, Biblical Ladders

PETER H LAWRENCE

MONARCH
BOOKS

First published by Monarch Books 1999

ISBN 1 85424 461 2

Editorial Office: Monarch Books,
Broadway House, The Broadway, Crowborough,
East Sussex TN6 1HQ

British Library Cataloguing Data
A catalogue record for this book is available
from the British Library.

Designed and produced for the publishers by
Bookprint Creative Services
P.O. Box 827, BN21 3YJ, England.
Printed in Great Britain.

To Roger, my best friend

ACKNOWLEDGEMENTS

Writing a book is very hard work and can be very tiring. I could never have done it without the help, skills and support of the following people.

A very big thank you to Melanie who typed the manuscript brilliantly and with lightning speed; the fastest keyboard-basher in the South. I am grateful to the parish of Canford Magna, and especially Anne and Sally, for permitting Melanie to do it in office time; to Liz for proof-reading it, Annie for correcting it and Roger and Mary for allowing me to bare their souls publicly; to Adele, Howard and Tony who have done wonders with pen, ink and computer. Finally thanks to Tony and Jane Collins, Carol and our girls, and God, for loving me.

I'm off for a rest now.

Peter H. Lawrence

Contents

VITAL INFORMATION

The game

When the board-game 'Snakes and Ladders' was first published in Britain in 1892, the Victorians were very pleased with its moral aspects. The meekness ladder led to goodness, and diligence to reward, while the cruelty snake led to punishment, pride to a fall, and so on.

In biblical snakes and ladders the game of life is slightly different. Jesus is the ladder (John 1:51), Satan is the snake (Revelation 12:9), the aim is heaven and everyone who finds Jesus wins the game.

The book

I have included material from Genesis, the first book of the Bible, to Revelation, the final one. I hope everyone will benefit from a brief overview of the Christian Scriptures. In the process we encounter snakes and ladders and the way which leads to God, the Father.

Jesus appears throughout the book. According to the Bible, Jesus did not come into existence at the start of the New Testament but 'existed before creation began' (Colossians 1:15 J B Phillips). As we look through the eyes of the New Testament it is possible to see Jesus walking through the pages of the Old Testament. He is involved in making the universe at the beginning (Hebrews 1:2) and the new creation at the end (Revelation 21:5,6; 22:13,16). Paul informs us that Christ 'accompanied' Moses in the Exodus from Egypt (1 Corinthians 10:4) and Peter writes about how the 'Spirit of Christ' was in the prophets (1 Peter 1:11). Jesus' presence is promised, prefigured and prophesied in the Old Testament section and at times experienced. When we come to the New Testament we find that his death, resurrection, ascension, baptising in the Holy Spirit and second coming fulfil all Old Testament hopes, dreams, wildest dreams and beyond. This book is primarily about this Jesus.

There are also Bible study questions for housegroups, notes for leaders, cryptic questions for fun-lovers, and seventy sermon topics for preachers.

The musical

Roger Jones has written the Christian musical *Snakes and Ladders* which covers similar ground to the book. From time to time we have worked together but neither publication is dependent on the other. I always try to illustrate biblical truth with examples and application from everyday life so it seemed appropriate in this book to include relevant stories about Roger and his family.

The symbols

I have used a few symbolic pictures at various points for edification and interest, to highlight various themes and to act as easy-to-find reference points. If you want to locate information about Jesus then look for the crown of thorns; if you want to read about Roger then hunt out the keyboard; and if you're keen to obtain a summary of the Bible then follow the good book. The following key explains all the symbols.

Biblical story – from beginning to end; Genesis to Revelation.

 Snakes – I apologise to ophiophilists but all the snakes in this book are nasty except one or two which are wise as serpents and really ladders in disguise.

 Ladders – As with the board-game you don't have to climb any of them – they are more like escalators that work by grace once you're on the first step – but all of them are good except one which is really a nasty snake in ladder's clothing.

 Covenants . . . in Scripture are solemn agreements which establish a firm relationship between God and his people. The five major ones from the Bible are covered in these pages.

 Judgement – In this book the baddies always lose and the goodies always win, eventually – because of Jesus.

 Christophanies . . . are appearances of Christ to people. The Jesus sandals indicate five possible Old Testament ones which readers can decide about for themselves.

 Bible Studies – for groups, on John's Gospel, eleven of them, with questions, answers and notes for leaders. You may wonder why they are all on John's Gospel. I like John's Gospel.

Appendices – four of them, for preachers, with ideas for seventy different sermons.

 Roger Jones . . . is a Christian composer who keeps cropping up to help me illustrate and apply biblical truth.

 The Church – we have branches everywhere.

Jesus . . . is mentioned in every chapter. It's all about Jesus.

1 THE PERSON WHO CAN THROW THE BIGGEST NUMBER STARTS

In the beginning God

Roger Jones and I flew into Heathrow – by car. We were late. My fault partly. My mother has lived near the airport since 1959. You would have thought I'd be able to find it without getting lost . . . but. . . .

The other 'partly' was an accident on the M25. Traffic jammed every which way. We queued and prayed, queued and prayed, got there, thanked my friend for the lift, raced in through the automatic doors, checked in the baggage, were allocated the last two places on the plane, thanked God, and took off.

Roger likes planes and travelling. His little legs fit nicely under the seat in front, and his pleasant manner gets him whatever he wants from the hostesses. We arrived safely in Montreal and waited patiently by the carousel for our luggage.

Roger's two massive cases came sliding around one after the other containing enough clothes for his ten-day tour and an abundance of cassettes, CDs and musical scores written by himself. While Roger was away paying his dues everybody else's cases appeared and were duly claimed. Eventually the motor stopped as Roger appeared from customs with a receipt and a suitcase in each hand.

'All right then?' he asked in a Brummie accent.

'My case hasn't arrived,' I replied.

'Oh! You'll be able to carry one of mine then,' he said, with a smile.

We reported it and went on to our hosts arriving at 9pm in Canada and 2am in me. A banquet with important guests was waiting for the famous composer, so Roger put on a jacket and tie and went to join them while I put on a plastic smile.

Montreal was beautiful. Sunshine, frost, water everywhere, suspension bridges, autumnal colours Canadian style – and black squirrels. Roger conducted the choir, I sold the music, tapes and CDs and then we flew to Ottawa over more incredible scenery. Just after we left, my suitcase arrived in Montreal.

Ottawa is something else. Everywhere we wandered brought us into contact with clean streets, impressive buildings, manicured parks and well-maintained canals while all the unsightly cables we found in other Canadian cities were hidden underground. It's a showpiece which befits the historic capital of one of the largest countries in the world. Situated at the confluence of the Ottawa, Gatineau and Rideau rivers the views we found on a sunny, still, cold day peering through colourful maple leaves now look very special in our photo albums. It's a shame we couldn't stay until winter because then they lower the level of the canals to two feet and many people skate to work on a regular basis for several months. Having always enjoyed the old Dutch painters' portrayal of happy skaters in the middle of snowy European landscapes I'd like to have witnessed the Canadian equivalent, but we had work to do.

Roger played, they sang and I sold what I could. My suitcase arrived in Ottawa, just after we'd left for Vancouver.

We arrived late on Saturday night.

'Roger, you'll be preaching at the 11am service here,' his host informed us. 'Plenty of time for a good night's sleep and a leisurely bath in the morning.'

'Fine,' said Roger, 'and what is Peter doing?'

'Ah yes,' he continued rather more slowly. 'Peter is preaching on the Island. Needs to be up at five for the early boat.'

It was stunning. Scottish-type mist peeling away with the dawn to reveal the Coast Mountains and a sea bespotted with tall-tree islands. Paradise can't improve much on this except perhaps for a freshly-laundered white robe and a good night's sleep (Revelation 7:13).

Vancouver has everything we don't have in Dorset. The fortunate tourist can enjoy the sight of eagles, whales, mountains, giant trees, tower-blocks, suspension bridges, ski-slopes and black squirrels. We sold some more books and tapes before we flew to Toronto and this time my suitcase arrived before we left. I was able to take it with me.

Roger was met at the airport and whisked away in a posh car for his evening meal and session. John Arnott, from the Vineyard at Stratford-upon-Avon, was supposed to be meeting me, but no one was there. The much publicised outpouring of God's blessings hadn't arrived yet at the churches John pastored and life seemed altogether more laid-back and relaxed. I rang him up as I was due to speak at 8pm.

'Oh! Thought you'd make your own way, Peter,' he said nonchalantly.

'Is it far?' I asked.

'No, not far, about a hundred kilometres,' he replied.

That's a Canadian 'not far', I thought to myself.

'Would you suggest bus, taxi, train or huskies?' I enquired in my best English accent.

'Try this phone number,' John suggested and I jotted it down. When I finally got through I was told they couldn't help me themselves but they'd try and find someone who could. 'I'll be stood outside,' I said. 'Wearing a dog-collar.'

Time passed by. A lady walked straight towards me at about 6.30pm so I thrust my neck hopefully in her direction but she ignored me and went into the airport. At about 7.15pm she came out and asked if I was Peter Lawrence. Apparently no one told her what a dog-collar looked like and she must have thought I'd be in front of a kennel.

My new young acquaintance was rather nervous, having just passed her driving test and never having driven on a free-way before, but she performed well at the wheel and we arrived at 9pm. I did my bit at the meeting and afterwards relaxed into the luxury of clean pyjamas in a bed they managed to find for me.

John and Carol Arnott gave me coffee in the morning before sending me back to Toronto. 'Nothing much ever happens here,' he said. 'It's desperately hard work. We've just opened up another meeting place at the airport; not many so far but we keep trying. Do you think you might have a word with John Wimber to see if he could visit us and encourage us?' How times have changed! The so-called 'Toronto Blessing' arrived at the Airport Fellowship just over two years later in the January of 1994.

Roger and I had a day to ourselves at the end of the tour so we caught a bus down to the American border. It was amazing. Having viewed the dazzling beauty of Canadian cities in their autumnal glory we'd already seen enough spectacular sights to last a lifetime but this was definitely the champagne at the celebration. The American Falls would have been majestic enough on their own but the Horseshoe ones were awesome.

People view Niagara Falls from many places and angles. The boats take you close up and underneath; helicopters hover near the surface; steps and lifts take you down behind; a revolving restaurant gives you the panoramic view from above and at night they're lit up with coloured spotlights. My favourite place is the path by the fence where the rapids gather before tumbling over the precipice. From just a few feet away you can easily imagine you're going over in a barrel.

It's a breathtakingly gorgeous place which attracts honeymoon couples from all over the world, but it's also a place of power that you don't mess with unless you're Superman. The creation reflects something of the creator.

'And to think,' I said to Roger. 'God knocked this up in six days as a temporary measure. Heaven is going to be something special.'

Facts of creation

The visual impact of creation can be addictive. Hundreds of people regularly travel thousands of miles to see the natural wonders of the world. We browse through travel brochures during the long nights of the winter months and dream of days on sun-kissed white beaches with exotic birds twittering in zephyr-tossed palm trees. The thought of such romantic and even escapist experiences excites us all, but as I found recently, while researching a sermon, staying at home and looking up the facts and figures of creation can prove to be almost as inspiring. I discovered this information in various books on the shelves of our vicarage.

The sun is a star supporting a number of planets and satellites like the many other stars in the sky. Apart from our sun the nearest star to the earth is about four light years away. This means when we look out on a clear night at the twinkling lights we are not only seeing billions of miles but also looking into the past. We never see stars as they are today but only as they were years ago.

Light travels at 186,282 miles every second. I tried to use my calculator to work out the distance from the earth to the nearest star but it wasn't big enough so I asked my wife Carol. She has degrees in physics, is just as efficient as a computer, but far more pulchritudinous. The answer came back quickly: 5,865,696,000,000 miles away.

That is the nearest star to us in our galaxy. I looked up our galaxy, the Milky Way, in the *National Geographic Atlas of the World* and this is what I found. 'It is a gravitationally bound, rotating congregation of hundreds of billions of stars.' We have a rotating congregation which I sometimes think is gravitationally bound, but we don't have that many stars. According to the *Encyclopaedia Brittanica*, the nearest galaxy to our own is 10,000,000 light years away and 'today we know it is only one of billions of galaxies'. As John Lennon once wrote, I felt 'humbled, fat and small'.

The statistics are equally impressive when we return to our planet and focus on the other end of the scale. The *Superbook of Amazing Facts* states: 'It has been estimated that the number of living things occupying the earth, not including human beings, is in the region of 3000 quintillion.'

Carol says it looks like this:
3,000,000,000,000,000,000,000,000,000,000,000.

Being married to someone who did her second degree in nuclear physics has not always been as useful to me in my ministry as it was on this occasion. I asked her how many atoms there are in a drop of water. 'Ten to the power of ten,' she said, which apparently looks like this: 10,000,000,000. Of course atoms are made up of particles and particles are made up of quarks but that will probably do for now. The universe is very big, very small and very impressive.

The creator

Lo within a manger lies he who built the starry skies

Children as well as adults love to ask 'how big' or 'how small' but in my experience they also long to know *'how?'* How did it all come into being? Who threw the biggest number at the beginning and started the game of life? In many ways it is the most important question of the three because it has eternal significance for all of us. The Bible gives us this answer:

Jesus made it. The whole jolly lot. *Ex nihilo.* Out of nothing. Before he came to the earth and freely chose to limit himself for a season in time and space.

Consider these verses carefully.

St Peter refers to Jesus as 'The author of life' (Acts 3:15).

St Paul writes of Jesus: 'By him all things were created: things in heaven and on earth . . . all things were created by him and for him' (Colossians 1:16).

The author of the letter to the Hebrews records that, through Jesus, God 'made the universe' (Hebrews 1:2).

Jesus was present in the beginning. He was the one by whom and through whom all things were made.

St John picks up this theme and extends it even further in his Gospel. Normally in church we speak of God the Father, God the Son and God the Holy Spirit in that order, but in John's Gospel we start with Jesus. As the story unfolds, Jesus makes the Father known to his disciples and to the world (John 10:30; 14:7-9), and towards the end he personally baptises his disciples in the Holy Spirit (John 20:22). In John everyone gets to know God the Father and God the Holy Spirit through Jesus and it is in John we find the clearest presentation of the claims of Christ.

Jesus talks about himself as existing 'before the world

began' (John 17:5) and 'before the creation of the world' (John 17:24). John refers to Jesus initially as the 'Word'. He describes his human birth like this: 'The Word became flesh and made his dwelling among us' (John 1:14). This is a title also used for Jesus in the book of Revelation. 'The name by which He is known is the Word of God' (Revelation 19:13; J B Phillips).

Seeing Jesus as 'the Word' now helps us to understand the first three verses of John's Gospel. 'In the beginning was the Word, and the Word was with God, and the Word was God. He was with God in the beginning. Through him all things were made; without him nothing was made that has been made' (John 1:1-3). This is all in keeping with what Peter, Paul and the author of Hebrews have already claimed for Jesus elsewhere in the New Testament. According to the Bible the universe was made by Jesus, through Jesus and for Jesus thus enabling us to call Jesus 'creator'.

Billions of galaxies in the universe; quintillions of creatures on the earth; squillions of quarks in a drop of water. Stars, animals and H_2O. This Jesus who arrived beneath the brightest star, beside the stable animals through the broken waters of human birth, made everything there is. It is an astounding claim, and yet there is more to come.

The incarnate deity

Veiled in flesh the Godhead see

If we delve into the Greek text of John's Gospel we find that not only can we use the title 'creator' for Jesus but he also has the name which is above every other name.

When God appeared to Moses on the holy mountain in Arabia through a burning bush, Moses asked, 'Who shall I say called?' or words to that effect. God said to Moses, 'I AM who I AM. This is what you are to say to the Israelites: "I AM has sent me to you"' (Exodus 3:14).

The unique name above every other name for God is 'I AM'. In the Hebrew of the Old Testament it is written as 'Yahweh'; in the Greek of the New Testament it is '*EGO EIMI*'. God has many different names in the Bible such as 'the Lord', which is a descriptive term (there are other 'lords' in the Bible and in the world), but his real name, his unique name, is 'I AM'. It is the name Jesus takes for himself and is found at least fifteen times in John's Gospel if you read it carefully in the Greek.

Many people are aware of the Magnificent Seven in which Jesus declares, 'I AM – the bread of life (John 6:35); the light of the world (John 8:12); the gate (John 10:9); the good shepherd (John 10:11); the resurrection and the life (John 11:25); the way, the truth and the life' (John 14:6), and 'the true vine' (John 15:1-5).

Admittedly, the 'I AM's (*EGO EIMI*) would not be claims to divinity purely on linguistic grounds if it were not for the sentences which follow. These two make the point most clearly.

Jesus said, 'I am the resurrection and the life. He who believes in me will live, even though he dies; and whoever lives and believes in me will never die' (John 11:25-26). Jesus answered, 'I am the way and the truth and the life. No-one comes to the Father except through me' (John 14:6).

Jesus sets himself up as the answer to all humankind's needs and problems now and in all eternity and this is the reason for the '*EGO EIMI*' beginning of these and the other five 'I AM' statements. An oft-quoted summary by C S Lewis suggests that these are not the words of a good teacher or even a good man but can only be the words of a madman, a bad man or God himself.

But there are eight more 'I AM's hidden in the Greek text of John's Gospel which many people miss; a further eight which show even more clearly that Jesus takes the name of 'God' for himself. They are all worth a brief look if only to give us something to share with the Jehovah's Witnesses next time they call at the door, but for now here are the three most dramatic ones. (The fifteen 'I AM's are listed in Appendix 1. Here and in the Appendix I have used the NIV except for '*EGO EIMI*' which I have translated myself as 'I AM'.)

1. The first one comes after Jesus withdrew to a mountain by himself and the disciples decided to go home by boat. Suddenly the weather changed as winds began to whip through the narrow tunnel-like passes between the hills and concentrated all their venom on Lake Galilee. The experienced fishermen were taken by surprise and their paltry rowing powers rendered useless by the strength of such created forces. It was evening and their hope of reaching their destination by nightfall, if at all, was now greatly threatened by the storm – until they saw him, the creator, cutting a channel through the waves and walking on the rough waters towards them.

'They were terrified but he said to them, "I AM [*EGO EIMI*], don't be afraid"' (John 6:20). Matthew wrote, 'Those who were in the boat worshipped him' (Matthew 14:33).

2. The Temple in Jerusalem was the centre of the Jewish religion and the place which symbolically expressed the presence of God. Near the place where the offerings were put Jesus was challenged by the Pharisees who simply could not accept his claims to be from God.

'"I tell you the truth," Jesus answered, "before Abraham was born, I AM [*EGO EIMI*]". At this they picked up stones to stone him, but Jesus hid himself, slipping away from the temple grounds' (John 8:58,59).

3. Jesus escaped their grasp in James Bond style because his time had not yet come, but in due course the moment for the sacrifice arrived. It was night when the soldiers and officials

from the chief priests and Pharisees came for Jesus carrying torches, lanterns and weapons – led by Judas, the Apostle. This time there was no escape as Jesus chose to stand there, face them and reveal his identity.

'"I AM [*EGO EIMI*]," Jesus said . . . When Jesus said, "I AM [*EGO EIMI*]" they drew back and fell to the ground' (John 18:6).

Jesus' ability to save his disciples (1) is matched by his capability to thwart the enemy (2 and 3) and on all three occasions he assumes the title of God, I AM. Each time the power which is displayed and the response of those present indicates the claim of Christ to be God – I AM – *EGO EIMI*.

The climax of the gospel confirms all that has gone before as the ex-doubter addresses the Lord Jesus.

'Thomas said to him, "My Lord and my God"' (John 20:28).

Jesus received Thomas' affirmation of his divinity. Whatever we choose to do with the claims of Jesus in John's Gospel, they are unmistakable. Jesus made the universe and Jesus is God.

John begins and ends his gospel with Jesus. It's all about  Jesus. He presents him as the source of life and the answer to life; indeed as life itself. Our human expressions of Christianity as found in the church, though building on this unique foundation, are often clumsy, sometimes boring and always inadequate. But behind the cathedrals and village churches, the cassocks, hassocks and solemnity is a long, ancient catalogue of changed lives which continually give testimony to someone very real and special. His name is Jesus, I AM, God in human form, the creator.

GROUP STUDY *In the beginning*

There are notes at the back of the book to help group leaders answer these questions.

A trick question: What is greater than the love of God, worse than the judgement of hell, and if you eat it leaves you starving?

Read John 1:1-14.

1. Who made the world? (Acts 3:15; Colossians 1:16; Hebrews 1:2; John 1:1-3).
2. Who is Jesus? (John 20:28). Who made Jesus?
3. Why do you think the world did not recognise him? (John 1:10. See John 3:19).
4. Why do you think 'his own', who knew the Old Testament, did not receive him? (John 1:11. See John 10:30-33).
5. In the Bible the glory of God is the discernible presence of God. What do you think John meant when he wrote, 'We have seen his glory?' (John 1:14).
6. Verse 14 says that Jesus became flesh – became one of us. It also describes him as the 'One and Only'. So, in what ways was Jesus like us, the same as us – and in what ways was he different from us – unique?
7. How may we become children of God? (John 1:12–13).

2 THE FIRST LADDER IS VERY HIGH

In the image of God

On two wintry occasions I have been the seasonal English chaplain in Zermatt, high up in the Swiss Alps beside the Italian border. No cars were allowed and only the sound of horse-drawn sleighs with jingly bells disturbed the still, frozen air. Wrapped up well and snuggled under the heavy blankets, you could slide gently along the crisp snow and see some of the highest mountains in Europe. The Dom (14,911ft) is the highest one entirely in Switzerland; the Monte Rosa (15,203ft) is the tallest in Italy/Switzerland combined; but both are overshadowed by a smaller peak (14,692ft) which appears on every postcard, table-mat, jumper, painting, bag or tea tray which can be bought from the village shops. Standing upright, pointing to the sky like a Turkish scimitar, is the mountain which kills more would-be mountaineers than any other. Skiing from Switzerland into Italy and back again in a day beside the brutally rugged Matterhorn is a memory I shall always treasure.

I've climbed Scafell Pike, Snowdon and Ben Nevis in sunshine and mist. I once found a few cloudless days to drive through the hills of Wales and parts of Ireland, spent a sunny fortnight in the Scottish highlands and after several attempts encountered a clear blue sky at Keswick. Our little hills are as picturesque as most when the sun shines. I've driven through the Dolomites of Italy, the Coast Mountains of Canada, the Sierra de Bernia in Spain, flown over Kilimanjaro in Tanzania and skied among the Swiss Alps. They are tremendous, every one of them, but as yet the Drakensberg Mountains in South Africa top the others for me. They are that much more severe, rugged and dramatic, especially when the low setting sun plays light tricks on the different surfaces. But though they are all very high, some members of God's creation are capable of climbing higher still.

Creatures with wings who live in 'rocky cathedrals' can soar above most of the mountain summits I have seen. In my travels I have been fortunate enough to encounter fish-eagles swooping in Africa, bald-headed eagles scavenging in Canada and golden ones soaring in northern Britain. Recently, as we returned from Builth Wells in central Wales, a large, almost eagle-sized, russet-coloured bird of prey with fingered feathers, flew slowly in front of our car enabling us to see it at close range. It was sensational; a red kite, so I'm told.

We are made in the image of God

In my life I've been greatly blessed to see some of the high mountain peaks and the birds of prey which rise above them but, according to the Bible, the highest point of all visible creation is you and me.

> Then God said, 'Let us make man in our image, in our likeness, and let them rule over the fish of the sea and the birds of the air, over the livestock, over all the earth, and over all the creatures that move along the ground.'
> So God created man in his own image, in the image of God he created him; male and female he created them.
>
> (Genesis 1:26–27)

Not only are we made to be the rulers of earth, the kings and queens of our majestic planet, but higher still. We are made in the image of God, who is spirit (John 4:24). It's as if we began our earthly life on the highest rung of God's creation ladder.

Genesis goes on to record how it was done: 'The Lord God formed the man from the dust of the ground and breathed into his nostrils the breath of life, and the man became a living being' (Genesis 2:7).

Most of the Hebrew words used for 'breath' can also mean 'spirit' and the one used here is no exception. This is what gives us life. This is the part made in the image of God. Adam and Eve had communion with God as he spoke to them person to person; God's Spirit to their spirits. They were in harmony with God, with one another and with the world.

Zechariah summarises the major achievements of the creator like this: 'The Lord, who stretches out the heavens, who lays the foundation of the earth, and who forms the spirit of man within him' (Zechariah 12:1).

The facts and figures of creation and some of its unbelievable beauty can leave us motionless in wonder, but the truth that God is spirit and we are made in his image is awesome.

To be made in the image of God with a spirit qualifies us to enter a world even more thrilling than the one of predators and peaks. The seen world, despite its solid appearance, is only temporary but the unseen spiritual world is the one which lasts for ever. 'So we fix our eyes not on what is seen, but on what is unseen. For what is seen is temporary, but what is unseen is eternal' (2 Corinthians 4:18).

The Bible majors on the spiritual side of humankind and this spirituality can also be experienced to some degree in the world. The evidence for the existence of the spiritual world can be found in the innate spiritual desires of human beings particularly in contrast to some of the other beings in God's created order. God permits us to kill and eat other animals but not human beings because they are made in the image of God (Genesis 9:6). The difference, therefore, between ourselves and other creatures is seen to be the spirit which is made in God's likeness. For those who have eyes to see, the invisible spiritual world to which we belong is very real.

Worship

From earliest times we find evidence that humankind has an inbuilt yearning to worship. Every civilisation has its gods and religions including the first cave dwellers who left behind their wall-paintings which depict various kinds of pantheistic worship and idolatry. Religion has been a world-wide phenomenon ever since, and even today the secular world has its own gods. Those who don't go to churches often go to sports fixtures, pop concerts or idolise their television heroes. Their desire to worship points to the existence of a spiritual impulse within all people.

There is no evidence of worship in the rest of the animal kingdom. This seems to be a spiritual yearning located only in men and women among earthly creatures.

Morality

In the societies of our world both today and in history there is a natural longing for peace, order and justice. 'It's not fair,' is the cry of every hard-done-by child all over the globe. Rules exist in every country normally along the lines of the greatest good for the greatest number. The moral teaching of the ancient Egyptians, Babylonians, Hindus, Chinese, Greeks and Romans are remarkably similar to one another and to the British sense of fair-play and justice which is still in evidence today. Whenever we quarrel and try to show how the other person is in error we suggest there is already some kind of agreement in existence about right and wrong. It is often called the 'law of human nature' which C S Lewis, in *Mere Christianity*, argues we do 'not share with animals or vegetables or inorganic things'.

Intelligent animals can be taught to do many things with a system of rewards and punishments, but a 'conscience' seems to be uniquely inherent in human beings. Morality is considered by many to be a characteristically human trait and I believe it is located in the spirit – the part which is made in the image of the truly moral God.

Imagination

Poetry, music, art, dance, theatre, books, sport and so many other human interests are what makes life worth living for many people. They provide the fun and laughter, pathos and stimulation which so many of us crave in our quest for affirmation, satisfaction and metaphysical truth. In contrast, animals seem more content with the daily round. I have always felt it strange to see sheep, cattle or horses with heads bowed, munching grass in front of majestic mountain scenery or beneath the most spectacular blazing sunset without ever pausing to look up.

In places where the presence of the spirit is denied, life can sometimes appear very dull. Malcolm Muggeridge was a newspaper reporter in Russia during its communist days, and he frequently made up news because there was none to report. He predicted at the time that he thought communism would eventually come to an end because it was 'so boring'.

The arts derive from our God-given drive to create, as children of the creator; a drive which comes from our vivid imaginations. To create, God had first to imagine. The sciences also emerge due to our ability to picture and dream what may yet be; an ability which has taken us from caves to palaces; from the earth to the moon and back; from animal to human existence. I believe our natural desire and ability to create belongs to our spiritual nature.

Life after death

Around the world in every land and every culture and throughout history we find cemeteries. Whether we look at the pyramids of Egypt, the happy hunting ground of the American Indians or the Valhalla of Scandinavia, we find a human interest and belief in life after death. I have taken many funerals in my time for church and non-church people and found the hope of eternity to be a 'normal' human characteristic within all who mourn. In contrast there appears to be no evidence in the rest of the animal kingdom for funeral rites or an interest in life after death. This seems to be confined to those who have a spirit.

The desire to worship, to be kind and good, to imagine and create and to live for ever are our birth rights as children made in the image of God. The creation speaks of the creator and the spirit cries out for God. All four of these natural human longings are discernible in humankind and point to the presence of a spirit within each of us. The first three, worship, morality and the imagination, contribute towards a higher quality of living. Life with a zing. The fourth one, eternity, offers the hope of life in a new dimension way beyond our wildest dreams. Living on after death is an idea worth taking very seriously.

The natural longing for post-mortem survival which we find in our world and in our spirits is answered by the revelation of Scripture. The Teacher in the book of Ecclesiastes says this: 'Remember him – before the silver cord is severed . . . and the dust returns to the ground it came from, and the spirit returns to God who gave it' (Ecclesiastes 12:6-7).

The spirit – the important part, the real part, the eternal part – returns to God at death.

In Luke chapter eight Jesus raises Jairus' daughter from the dead. At the point when life comes back to the little girl Luke records: 'Her spirit returned' (Luke 8:55). The implication is that her spirit survived the death of her body and simply returned at Jesus' command.

Jesus' own death is equally significant. Luke records Jesus' words at the moment of his death: 'Father, into your hands I commit my spirit' (Luke 23:46). Matthew and John both say he 'gave up his spirit' (Matthew 27:50; John 19:30). Jesus' resurrection appearances, historically affirmed by many, add considerable substance to the idea that Jesus' spirit survived death.

Luke also records Stephen's death in a similar way. 'But Stephen, full of the Holy Spirit, looked up to heaven and saw the glory of God, and Jesus standing at the right hand of God . . . Stephen prayed, "Lord Jesus, receive my spirit"' (Acts 7:55, 56, 59).

The New Testament implies that Jairus' daughter, Jesus and Stephen all possess a spirit which survived physical death. People are made in the image of God. We have a spirit. Unlike the mountains and the eagles we are stamped with eternity.

Jesus is the image of true humanity

Adam and Eve were made in the image of God with God's Spirit breathed into their nostrils but they never discovered how good that might have been. They upset the apple-cart and sinned as all those coming after them have continued to do, except one. The only person we can look at to see what it means to be fully human, as God intended us to be, is Jesus. When he became flesh he was like us in every way yet without sin (Hebrews 4:15). Just as God breathed his Spirit into Adam and Eve so the Holy Spirit came on Jesus at his baptism and remained with him (John 1:33). From then on we see before us in John's Gospel a second Adam who reveals to us what it is like to be a real man (1 Corinthians 15:22,45).

Jesus was angry (John 2:16), thirsty (John 4:7), and in need of food (John 4:31); he wept (John 11:35), was in pain (John 19:28), bled and died (John 19:30-34), but he was not weak, wet or wimpish. He was a leader whom men followed, a teacher who attracted crowds, a discerning counsellor whom individuals sought, and the compassionate son of a grieving mother.

The Son of Mary taught his disciples about loving one another and washed their feet (John 13:1-17). He impressed rich and famous (John 19:38-39), poor (John 9:35-38) and rejected (John 4:28-30), Jews, Samaritans and Gentiles. He loved Lazarus, blessed Mary Magdalene, helped Peter to face his pain, restored Thomas and inspired Nathaniel.

The Son of Man lived all his short life in a small country under the oppression of a greater power. He rarely travelled far, didn't write a book, and never made it into the influential societies of palaces, governments or universities. His closest friends betrayed him, denied him and deserted him and yet – given only three years by his Father in which to change the world – he made it. Today the world calculates its calendar dates in relation to Jesus' life.

There is an incredible height, breadth and depth to his love, knowledge and wisdom, even in adverse circumstances. On one occasion his enemies tried to trap him. 'Teacher,' they began, 'this woman was caught in the act of adultery. In the Law Moses commanded us to stone such women. Now what do you say?' (John 8:4-6).

This is quite brilliant. If Jesus lets them stone her then the love, compassion and forgiveness he has been teaching has to be abandoned, and the Romans will nail him for sanctioning an illegal execution. If he lets her go he has disobeyed God's laws as recorded in the Old Testament. Jesus' response is the stuff of film-writers' dreams. 'If any one of you is without sin,' he says, 'let him be the first to throw a stone at her' (John 8:7). This invitation from Jesus causes the people to condemn themselves and disperse, leaving him free to forgive the woman in the hope of her true repentance.

Jesus faced death more than once but, until the time was right, he escaped the lynch mobs. When the angry crowds tried to stone him on two separate occasions he somehow slipped away from them (John 8:59; 10:31-39). When they did come to arrest him, 'carrying torches, lanterns and weapons' (John 18:3), Jesus spoke and they all fell down (John 18:6). Jesus' dignity and courage left his accusers gasping. He was tried for his life before Pilate, but the Roman governor was the one who ended up being afraid and judged – by millions (John 19:8).

And then there are the signs which offer us another Magnificent Seven. Jesus turns water into wine (John 2: 1-11), heals a man who has been an invalid for thirty-eight years (John 5:5-9), feeds 5,000 with five loaves and two fishes (John 6:1-14), walks on the water in a strong wind (John 6:16-21), and gives sight to a man blind from birth, making use of the earth like God did in creation (John 9:6-7; Genesis 2:7). He heals a boy who is dying, from a distance (John 4:46-54), and brings a four-day-old corpse back to life by issuing instructions outside the tomb (John 11:43).

And at the heart of the most attractive personality of history, as recorded in John's Gospel, lies the key to the Spirit-filled spirit which unlocks the secret of abundant life. Matthew, Mark and Luke describe the stories of Jesus but John takes us behind the scenes to explain how it was all done.

The assumption many people make is that Jesus did all

these things because he was God, but that is not John's view. No other Gospel presents Jesus so clearly as God and yet no other Gospel presents Jesus as being so dependent upon his Father.

5:19   Jesus gave them this answer: 'I tell you the truth, the Son can do nothing by himself; he can do only what he sees his Father doing.'

8:28   Jesus said, 'I do nothing on my own but speak just what the Father has taught me.'

12:50   Jesus said, 'Whatever I say is just what the Father has told me to say.'

14:31   'The world must learn that I love the Father and that I do exactly what my Father has commanded me.'

15:15   'Everything that I learned from my Father I have made known to you.'

When the Son of God became flesh it would seem that he was no longer omnipresent (present everywhere), but located within a manger (John 1:14); no longer omnipotent (all-powerful), he could *do only* what the Father was doing (John 5:19); and no longer omniscient (all-knowing), but needed to *learn* things from the Father (John 8:28; 15:15).

Jesus' secret was in being a man with God's Holy Spirit breathed into his spirit enabling him to hear the Father, know the Father and do what the Father was doing. And the amazing promise Jesus makes is that because he was fully human we can do what he was doing.

'I tell you the truth, *anyone* who has faith in me will do what I have been doing' (John 14:12).

The Son of David demonstrates to us what a person with a spirit in union with God who is Spirit was intended to be like. For those made in the image of God it is what we can become in Christ because we are still the highest point of God's visible creation on earth. This means whenever a child is conceived a new eternal spirit with all this potential inside him or her comes into being, making it a very precious moment.

A new spirit

Harold and Winnie were married on cup final day, 1931. It was a very sad occasion. Harold was a Brum supporter all his life and West Brom beat Birmingham City 2-1. Interestingly they were in the cup final again on his silver wedding day and this time they lost 3-1 to Manchester City. All very sad but at least the Blues did get to Wembley in those days. The wedding part of both occasions, however, was a great joy.

Married life was fine until Harold and Winnie tried to become parents. They always wanted children but painfully for them tragedy followed tragedy as Winnie suffered a number of miscarriages, until eventually two boys were born alive. One lived a few hours and the other just a few days after which the doctor called Harold and Winnie into his surgery and gave them a little talk. Having looked at the medical records, the number of miscarriages and the deaths of the two boys born alive, he advised them not to try for any more children. He suggested it was not possible for Winnie to give birth to a child capable of survival and if they wanted a child it was better to consider adoption rather than keep enduring the anguish of these regular traumas.

A number of couples face such heartaches even today, but behind this very dark cloud is a little ray of sunshine which is worth considering. In the sad case of every miscarriage or child's death the Bible suggests that a new person has at least received the gift of spiritual life. Most Christian churches and most Christians are totally opposed to abortion in most circumstances. This is because we believe that at conception a human spirit is formed in the womb and an eternal person in the image of God has come into being. However damaged physically the child may be, however short a life he or she may live, this spirit returns to God at physical death and a person stamped with eternity has been created.

If the Christian Church, quite rightly, takes this line on abortion then it is also right to console the parents of miscarriages, still births and infant mortalities with some good news. It is not that they nearly became parents; it is not that we hope they may yet become parents; the truth is – they are parents. If they believe and trust in the Lord Jesus Christ then one day they will see their children face to face. A new body for everyone but the same spirit as on earth.

In 1940 Harold joined the British Army, left England and didn't return for six years. He was an architect who designed pubs for Ansells and if you've been to Birmingham you may well have visited one of them. Harold's skills were needed in India where he was involved in bridge-building for the troops and later in designing a hospital. For his efforts during the war Harold was awarded the British Empire Medal.

Coming home after it was all over was not a speedy process. Tidying up loose ends and waiting for an available boat to transport him around the Cape of Good Hope meant he did not return to England until 1946. In the autumn of 1947 Winnie discovered she was pregnant again. The doctor was dismayed but fortunately abortion was not considered an option in those days.

War is never good but it sometimes speeds up the advancement of science. There were also a few special coincidences in what occurred next which caused a number of people to believe with hindsight that Jesus was also involved.

Winnie was referred to the Queen Elizabeth Hospital in Birmingham where tests were carried out and careful notes made. It just so happened that one of the country's leading specialists was working on a new theory at the same time and was looking for a guinea pig on whom to test his thesis. In his lecturing travels (the QE is a teaching hospital), he came across Winnie's notes and asked to see her. The medical history fitted his research so he agreed to accept her as one of his patients providing she did all he told her to do. This meant diet, exercise, regular check-ups and obeying everything he said to the letter. Winnie agreed and all went as well as could be expected.

As the time for the delivery approached the specialist personally took control of all the preparations. He booked the date for the caesarean operation in his diary and made sure the right kind of incubator was ready nearby.

It was not an instant success. The little boy was removed alive and breathing but far from well and Harold and Winnie were told to expect the worst. The specialist, doctors and nurses did all they could. Harold never went to church but his wife was a bit more religious, while friends and relatives certainly did some praying.

It was touch and go for some time. Winnie told the hospital that if her son was going to die she wanted him home. One of the men at Ansell's brewery said, 'I don't know what we're going to do with Harold if he loses this one.' Sleep had to be grabbed in snatches. Aunty Nora came to visit and found them both asleep in the lounge where she fell asleep too. When they woke up to find Nora there, Winnie and Harold assumed it was bad news. 'Has he died?' Winnie asked.

But somehow the little boy hung on to life and after several months they were invited to come and take him home. When the Sister tried to hand him over he clung to her in panic, never having known his own parents, but gently, sensitively, they cradled him in their arms and took him home. A new human spirit had been born in the image of God and survived. The spirit of Roger William Jones was destined to help the Christian Church to dance and clap and sing.

The joy of human birth, when it is successfully completed, takes some beating. It is the highest visible rung on God's creation ladder.

GROUP STUDY *Born again of the Spirit*

A silly question: John the Baptist was filled with the Holy Spirit from birth and grew strong in spirit. What do John the Baptist, Attila the Hun and Winnie the Pooh have in common?

Read John 3:1-15.

1. How did Jesus perform miraculous signs? (John 3:2).
2. How can we see the kingdom of God? (John 3:3).
3. How can we enter the kingdom of God? (John 3:5).
4. How can our spirits come alive? (John 3:6).
5. What qualifies Jesus to speak of heavenly things? (John 3:31; 6:38).
6. How was the Son of Man lifted up? (John 3:14).
7. How may we be born again, enter the kingdom of God and receive eternal life? (John 3:15).

3 THE FIRST SNAKE IS VERY LOW
The fall

A crowd gathers in the porch of our church to shelter from the rain. They have arrived at the wedding but for now there isn't enough courage between them to come inside. I am alone in the warm, dry, friendly building; as afraid of them as they are of me.

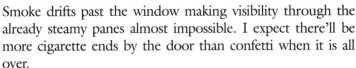

I can hear their nervous laughter like the noise in the bar from which they've just emerged. They wouldn't have made it this far without an alcoholic starter to dull the fear. Smoke drifts past the window making visibility through the already steamy panes almost impossible. I expect there'll be more cigarette ends by the door than confetti when it is all over.

I brave the elements and take my insecure frame bedecked

in cassock and surplice beyond the sanctuary and into the throng of threatening and threatened outsiders. I smile, I welcome, I crack jokes about Birmingham City to let them know I'm human and informed. I try to persuade them it's better inside than out but no one moves.

'It's OK Vic. We like the rain,' says the spokesman. 'One more smoke. We'll wait till she comes.'

When the bride does appear they don't take a second look. Her delayed arrival has merely been the stalling time they needed in order to stiffen the sinews and summon up the blood. Now, at the eleventh hour, huddled together in a close-knit group they cross the threshold of the church. If one of them is going to be struck down they are all going to be struck down together.

The big, brawny, manual-working community of East Birmingham who would never dream of backing away from a fight are somehow afraid of church, of the vicar and of God. Despite their fears we share a good service together.

Many people in Britain want what is good for themselves and their families. They are saddened and sometimes shocked at the bad news which they see on television and in the papers. They are ashamed when they err badly and carry guilt regularly to the doctors when they've let others down but they do not go to church. Christian meetings offer what so many people are seeking: forgiveness, mercy and peace with God; but still they stay away in their droves.

Today undertakers are finding a similar attitude towards funerals as I encountered at weddings. A former colleague of mine does a lot of 'non-Christian' funerals for the mourners who don't want a church service or the local vicar and in such cases my friend is asked to visit in a jacket and tie. They always like him, nearly always believe in God and life after death and 'yes', 'the Lord's my Shepherd' and 'the Lord's Prayer' would be fine. They don't often notice his clerical collar or robes at the service, because he's now a friend, but it has been a struggle to get them this far.

Life behind a dog-collar can be very revealing. I once visited a lady from our church who was married to an unbeliever. As I opened the gate and prepared to walk down the path I heard a loud, surprised, panicking voice shout 'Cor! B***** hell! It's the Vicar. I'm off,' and the back door slammed shut behind him. I wanted to shout after the husband, 'No! Actually I represent the other side,' but I was too late as he moved very quickly. In a crowded pub the collar always gets me an empty table to myself and yet in many shops I receive ten per cent off – for the church. When paying for something by cheque the banker's card is rarely needed. 'If we can't trust you Vicar, who can we trust?' they ask rhetorically with a smile.

It amazes me that people respect me and trust me with material things because of my collar but when it comes to spiritual things and I try to tell them about the true nature of God, they run a mile and don't trust me at all. Somehow the image of God has been distorted in their spirits and most people choose to stay away from the God of love because of fear.

Having been a church-goer all my life I've never really known why. I see fear and uncertainty in their eyes and body-language but don't fully understand it. Are they afraid of being got at? Of embarrassment? Of reproof? Of their own uneasy consciences? Of facing honest doubt? Whatever the symptoms the story of the fall highlights the root of all our fears. Whether we see Genesis 1–11 as a series of parables or historical fact the message of the Bible's first few chapters takes us all to the source of the problem.

Satan distorts the image of God

Adam and Eve were made in the image of God, king and queen of all they surveyed, and it was very good (Genesis 1:31). 'You and me and God' provided the perfect triangle. Within its three-cornered boundaries there was harmony, wholeness, love and peace with God and his world, with one another and with their own innermost beings. Adam and Eve were created for this but they were not the only beings God made with a spirit and they were not the only ones in the Garden of Eden.

You were in Eden, the garden of God; every precious stone adorned you: ruby, topaz and emerald, chrysolite, onyx and jasper, sapphire, turquoise and beryl. Your settings and mountings were made of gold; on the day you were created they were prepared. You were anointed as a guardian cherub, for so I ordained you. You were on the holy mount of God; you walked among the fiery stones. You were blameless in your ways from the day you were created till wickedness was found in you.

(Ezekiel 28:13-15)

A magnificent cherub was also in the garden with Adam and Eve. It is such a pity that modern culture has depicted cherubs as flying babies with bows and arrows because this is not the picture of them in the Bible. In the Old Testament two cherubs are made for the holy of holies to go either side of the ark of the covenant; overlaid with gold they are fifteen feet high with a wingspan to match (1 Kings 6:23-28). Angels don't come much bigger or better or higher than this, but sadly the cherub in the garden still wanted to be upwardly mobile. He reached for the sky.

You said in your heart, 'I will ascend to heaven; I will raise my throne above the stars of God; I will sit enthroned on the mount of assembly, on the utmost heights of the sacred mountain. I will ascend above the tops of the clouds; I will make myself like the Most High.'

(Isaiah 14:13-14)

This was a big mistake and for him it became a rung too far. Wanting to become like God caused his tragic fall from grace and the fall was very great. Instead of mingling with the stars he landed on his face in the dust. 'How you have fallen from heaven, O Lucifer, son of the dawn! You have been cast down to the earth . . . you are brought down to the grave, to the depths of the pit.' (Isaiah 14:12,15. Adapted from KJV and NIV).

Apparently it came about as the result of a battle royal in heaven. God, himself, was not directly involved, but Archangel Michael and his troops were still too powerful.

 And there was war in heaven. Michael and his angels fought against the dragon, and the dragon and his angels fought back. But he was not strong enough, and they lost their place in heaven. The great dragon was hurled down – that ancient serpent called the devil, or Satan, who leads the whole world astray. He was hurled to the earth, and his angels with him.

(Revelation: 12:7-9)

How the mighty have fallen! The majestic cherub known as Lucifer or Satan who was virtually on top of the created-order-ladder for angels has now slipped off it altogether and become a snake. As a serpent seeking revenge he moves sinuously through the vegetation of the garden into the orchard where he hears God speaking to Adam.

'And the Lord God commanded the man, "You are free to eat from any tree in the garden; but you must not eat from the tree of the knowledge of good and evil, for when you eat of it you will surely die"' (Genesis 2:16-17).

Satan's strategy is always to oppose the will of God and now he puts this into practice. 'Did God really say?' (Genesis 3:1). A seed of doubt is sown. The image of God in the spirit is challenged. 'Did God really say, "You must not eat?"' (Genesis 3:1). How negative. Why not? If he was as loving as he said he'd let you eat anything – without restriction – allow freedom. This is prohibition – ball and chain, denial of rights, lack of liberties, treating adults like children.'

The image begins to change. A veil of deception distorts the picture. Perhaps God doesn't really love me after all.

'Eat one piece of fruit and you'll die? (Genesis 3:3). You can't be serious. That's Disney World, Snow White, for kids. You don't die by eating figs. God is telling you porky pies. How will you know if you don't try it? Bigoted people always make judgements without trying things for themselves.'

The God who is for us becomes the God who is against us. We're slipping down below the mountains and eagles now. We're ignoring the good fruit on every other tree. This is obsession – got to, must have, I'll never find out for sure unless . . .

The lust for knowledge leads to the betrayal of trust. The fruit of curiosity is irresistible. It is good for food, pleasing to the eye and desirable for gaining wisdom (Genesis 3:6).

Is salvation possible? Not now, the hour is too late. Many of the gains of the first ladder are lost as those who were meant to be the heirs of God's kingdom slide down the slippery snake. Their eyes are opened by the lick of a viper's tongue but the poisoned bite goes deep. God was right all along and the grim reaper awaits us all. Paradise is lost. The king and queen hand over their God-given authority to Satan who becomes the 'Prince of this world' (John 12:31; 14:30; 16:11).

Suddenly it's gone quite chilly. There is a need to cover up and hide. Where are the masks? The mirror image has cracked into a thousand pieces. I no longer want to hear God, to know him or to see him face to face. Who am I? Where can I go? Once I was the son of God in the garden of delight. I was loved, cherished and affirmed without fear or pain. Once I was under no condemnation. Now I'm restless. My spirit is lost. Where am I? I'm not here, Lord.

God appears as a man 'walking in the garden in the cool of the day' (Genesis 3:8). Several times in the Old Testament God appears as a man and many think it is not unreasonable to give him the same name as the God-man of the New Testament. Scholars call this a possible 'Christophany'. If this is one of those then it is Jesus, the judge, who confronts Adam and Eve.

'Who is to blame, Adam?'

'Her, Lord. The woman you put here with me.'

'Who is to blame, Eve?'

'The slippery serpent, Lord. I had no chance.'

Judgement is swift. Honest toil becomes irksome labour; the wonder of marriage becomes a matter of shame, lust and domination; the joy of bearing children becomes a source of physical anguish; and humankind's control over the animal kingdom becomes a matter of danger and brute force. The shrewd symbol of primeval chaos is cursed and destined to crawl on its belly and grovel in the dust. The once magnificent angel is condemned to struggle with mere mortals until one day he will be crushed beneath their feet. Until then the pain goes on (Genesis 3:14-19).

'Your desire will be for your husband, and he will rule over you' (Genesis 3:16). Many people when questioned describe women's identity in relation to their husbands. I am married to the rector's wife. And most men when questioned about who they are answer in terms of the job they do. I am the rector.

'Painful toil . . . all the days of your life' (Genesis 3:17). Indeed. Sin spoils. Disharmony and dysfunction, disease and decease enter in. We fall out of sync with the world, with one another, with ourselves and with God.

But though the slide down Satan's back is a very great fall, it is not back to the beginning and the game is far from over. At the moment of curse and judgement prophetic hope appears. The judge predicts his own future role as the serpent's 'head-banger'. 'I will put enmity between you and the woman, and between your offspring and hers; he will crush your head, and you will strike his heel' (Genesis 3:15). The woman's offspring will crush the head of Satan. One day the Son of Mary will deliver from the power of sin some of the fallen sons and daughters of Eve.

The deposed royal family are driven from the garden of God and more cherubim are drafted in to guard the way to the tree of life. What a shame Adam and Eve responded with blame-shifting rather than honesty. Who knows how different life might have been for them and for us if they had faced the pain and come to God humbly for help?

A wrong image of God drives us away from God

Someone else wanted to run away from the Lord as well as Adam and Eve but in the end he found healing through a different response. Peter was one of the first people to meet Jesus when his ministry began. The carpenter decided to give the trawler a fishing lesson and told him to 'put out into deep water, and let down the nets for a catch' (Luke 5:4). Peter was not keen.

'Master, we've worked hard all night and haven't caught anything' (Luke 5:5), he objected. Then, maybe after a spirit-filled look from Jesus, he reluctantly agreed. 'But because you say so, I will let down the nets.'

Net result – so many fish the two boats began to sink.

Peter's response – 'Go away from me, Lord; I am a sinful man' (Luke 5:8).

This is right at the start of Jesus' ministry and Peter's reaction to seeing something of the glory of God revealed in Jesus is the same as Adam and Eve. The comment, 'Go away from me, Lord' (Luke 5:8) communicates something very similar to the description, 'they hid from the Lord God among the trees of the garden' (Genesis 3:8). 'I am a sinful man' is the big difference. Peter does not blame anyone else.

The wrong fear of God is the natural result of sin as people want to get away from God. Sin distorts the image of God in their spirits, letting in this negative emotion which causes them to try and flee from his presence.

Jesus gives us the right image of God

Putting this right, when given the opportunity, is where the image of Jesus is so helpful. Through reading the Gospel accounts of his life in the New Testament, Jesus can become familiar and by his Spirit he can be known. It is through Jesus that we discover what the Father is really like.

Jesus says, 'If you knew me, you would know my Father also' (John 8:19); 'Anyone who has seen me has seen the Father' (John 14:9); 'The Father is in me and I in the Father' (John 10:38); 'I and the Father are one' (John 10:30). Or as Paul puts it, Jesus 'is the image of the invisible God' (Colossians 1:15).

This is one of the most fundamental and important truths of Christianity; the Christmas story; the incarnation; Immanuel – God with us. Jesus reveals the Father to us. Jesus shows us what God is like. Jesus restores to us the true image of God which Adam and Eve lost through sin in the garden.

We are made in the image of God but when Adam and Eve sinned that image was distorted – they were ashamed; they ran away and hid; they were afraid of God. Ever since then humankind has been trying to get back into the garden of Eden: trying through good works and sacrifices; trying but failing; still afraid; still unsure; still with a distorted image of God within them.

If we look at the created world it is wounded, ecologically damaged, and maybe on its way out. If we look at humankind's world we see wars and rumours of wars, bloodshed, inhumanity and a fascination with evil. If we look at the Church it can sometimes appear in the mirror as a very spotty bride. If we look at our vicar, our mums and dads, our preachers, politicians and peers we shall see sinners, tarnished images, damaged people, hurting emotions, wrong actions and reactions. Complete holiness and righteousness is only a theory. None of us ever see or experience it totally in others.

There is only one person to look at if we want to know what God is like and that is Jesus. 'In these last days he has spoken to us by his Son . . . through whom he made the universe. The Son is the radiance of God's glory and exact representation of his being' (Hebrews 1:2-3).

Over the years I've done some Christian counselling and this is the place where many conversations lead: the distorted image of God. A harsh religious knowledge teacher, a blood and thunder evangelist, an abusive father, a low image of self or a phobia about living can all lead to a deep-seated fear of God; the one who'll get me if I make a mistake; the Gotcha God hiding behind a bush in the garden waiting to leap out at my least mistake and shout, 'Gotcha'.

Jesus shows us what the Father is like. Jesus helps us to have a right image of God the Father restored to our spirits.

Right at the end of John's Gospel, after the resurrection of Jesus, Peter is given another fishing lesson. This is similar to the one in Luke but significantly different. Once more they fish all night and catch nothing until, early in the morning, Jesus stands on the shore and tells them to throw their net on the right side of the boat. Again there is a large catch of fish but this time Peter's response is not the same as before: 'As soon as Simon Peter heard him say, "it is the Lord", he wrapped his outer garment around him (for he had taken it off) and jumped into the water. The other disciples followed in the boat' (John 21:7-8).

It looks as if this time Peter jumped in the water and swam towards Jesus. At the beginning of the Gospels Peter is afraid and wants to run away from Jesus but now, at the end of the

Gospels, Peter loves Jesus and wants to reach him as quickly as he can. Why? What has made the difference?

Was it because Peter had got his act together, taken holiness and righteousness seriously, and sinned much less? Far from it. He'd tried to kill someone with a sword (John 18:10), denied Jesus three times (John 18:15-18, 25-27) and called down curses on his own head (Mark 14:71). It doesn't get much worse than that. It seems much more evil than eating the wrong kind of fruit. In truth you couldn't think of a more difficult moment in his life for meeting Jesus.

The answer can only be that this time Peter knows Jesus. He knows *that when we sin the right thing to do is to move towards Jesus not away from him.* He has met 'Yahweh', 'I AM', face to face. He has seen the person and character of God the Father revealed in Jesus. The image of God which was distorted at the beginning of the Gospels has now been put right. Despite horrendous sins and serious crime he now 'jumps' to get to Jesus where he finds healing and restoration (John 21:7). Jesus can restore the right image of Father God to us.

Jesus can heal our distorted image of God

Pauline is a very fine pianist. At home she can play almost anything using music and her spirit flies. At church it has never been quite that easy. Traditional playing is OK. She follows the black dots with comfort and providing she is tucked away neatly in the corner normally copes competently.

Pentecostal playing, in which the pastor is the worship leader, is something quite different. He begins singing whatever song comes into his head while the pianist and other musicians are expected to know the song and key instantly and busk along merrily.

Pauline was put on the stage, centre spotlight, seated at an impressive grand piano before several hundred people. When the pastor began singing, she was expected to join in but failed and everybody's nightmare occurred. In front of a packed congregation Pauline froze and not a note was played. Roger Jones agreed to see her.

Brought up by a strict father in a strict church, Pauline had learnt at an early age that only her best was good enough for God and busking was not her best. Afraid of making a mistake, of letting God down, Pauline became paralysed by fear. 'This,' said Roger, 'is nothing to do with playing the piano. This,' he continued, 'is everything to do with your image of Father God.'

Pauline was very afraid of God. From an early age she was very much aware of the flames of hell where God sent people who did not believe in Jesus. This was something which needed to be tackled but it had to be done within the truths of Scripture. One day a picture was given which was a great help.

A blind man was walking towards a cliff edge. Jesus suddenly appeared and said, 'If you continue the way you are going you will fall off the edge of the cliff.' Jesus warns people about the cliff edge; Satan tries to lure people towards it and push them over.

For God did not send his Son into the world to condemn the world, but to save the world through him. Whoever believes in him is not condemned, but whoever does not believe stands condemned already because he has not believed in the name of God's one and only Son.

(John 3:17-18)

The picture of the blind man and Jesus was not Scripture but it was consistent with Scripture; it provided a helpful interpretation of Scripture. Hell is as real as the Bible says it is; the place of condemnation and eternal separation from God; but the character of God, his merciful nature, is to offer to save people from it, even to the point of death on a cross. It is

Satan who wants to send people to hell. This picture proved to be another step on the way to healing.

Pauline also wrote some poems in which God was frequently mentioned but the god portrayed in the well-written verse was not the God and Father of our Lord Jesus Christ; he was not even the God of the Old Testament; he was more like the god of other primitive religions who continually requires sacrifices. Pauline knew Jesus had paid the sacrifice once and for all and to realise this truth about the god in her poem was helpful.

The curse of 'only the best will do for God' needed to be broken. Roger often teaches that to try and play perfect music *only* is like trying to eat a croissant without making any crumbs. (Seeing Roger eating a croissant makes the point even more convincingly.) A phrase he often uses to accompany this teaching is also very valuable. 'If a thing's worth doing,' he says, 'it's worth doing badly.' Think about it.

All of these points were well received by Pauline and contributed to a change in her thought patterns, but the real turning point came when Roger helped her to talk about her own father. When he died, while Pauline was in her early twenties, an older Christian said, 'Do not cry. Crying at the funeral of a Christian is showing lack of faith.'

Oh dear! What some people say and teach. I would have thought in John chapter eleven Jesus showed more faith in God than anyone else before or since. To raise a four-day-old corpse is not bad going. Even so, 'Jesus wept' (John 11:35).

Roger listened and counselled Pauline, with others present, (it is not advisable to counsel someone of the opposite sex on a one-to-one basis), and then helped her to identify the grief. He prayed, 'Come Holy Spirit' and God came. Jesus immersed her in his love as Pauline wept for forty-five minutes. Later she said, 'It was so real it was as if it had just happened.' Jesus seemed to turn her emotional clock back to the moment of the original bereavement so that she could grieve now as she wanted to do then and be healed. In my opinion Pauline has played the piano beautifully in worship ever since.

The love and mercy of God housed in our spirits is always tarnished and soiled when we sin or are sinned against. The image of God is distorted and often we want to run away. The first snake in the Bible led to a very great fall for all humankind. At this stage in the game we have slithered down almost to the bottom but we are not without hope. The promise of the coming 'head-banger' is also there. *Jesus* is the one who can restore the right image of Father God to us and the game goes on.

GROUP STUDY *The image of the invisible God*

An interesting question: Who, in the New Testament, as well as Jesus, is called 'the Son of God?'
Read John 14:1-14.

1. How did Jesus' disciples know what God the Father was like? (John 14:9-11).
2. How did they know God the Father? (John 14:7).
3. How were they able to go to be with God the Father when they died? (John 14:1,6).
4. What helped them to believe in God the Father? (John 14:11. See also John 1:47-51; 2:11). What kind of experiences in life may stop us from believing in the right image of God?
5. How may we know what God the Father is like?
6. How may we know God the Father and go to be with him when we die? (John 14:6).
7. How may we help others to believe in God the Father? (John 14:12-14).

4 A LADDER BECOMES A SNAKE
As in the days of Noah

On a May day in 1998 I found myself sitting on a hard wooden pew for many hours. The building in which it was situated was old, tastefully preserved but cold and austere. The lofty ornate ceiling spoke of a bygone era when architects didn't worry about central heating and the tall arched windows seemed to point upwards to a higher authority beyond our reach. The welcome was not particularly warm but then the whole atmosphere was one of formality.

It was not a comfortable building and I was not comfortable. I wasn't quite sure why I'd come but I knew I had to be there as people who mattered thought my testimony might be useful. So I sat on solid oak and waited, just in case. During the coffee break I chatted to some locals who were keen to tell me about the particular room I was nervously waiting to enter.

'This', they said, 'is the actual court room where the murderers of Jamie Bulger were found guilty and sentenced.'

I remember that event well. When it came out on the national news, shivers went down the spine of virtually every parent in our land. My own daughters were quite young at the time and I gave all three of them a special hug that night. According to the newscaster, two young children took a toddler from a shopping precinct and killed him, and the nation's response was overwhelming. We were shocked. How could this be? Don't we all love children and aren't families precious to everyone in this country?

Sadly there is nothing new under the sun. I read in the newspaper recently of a seven-year-old girl who was hanged in England for being an accomplice to a murder in the year when our own Queen Mother was also seven years old. Apparently the little girl somehow assisted an eleven-year-old boy in committing this crime and they were executed together. Yes, it took place in England and yes, we the people of Britain hanged a seven-year-old girl in the twentieth century. Violence has been with us since the very first children were born.

A violent world

Adam and Eve produced several sons and daughters but their first two, Cain and Abel, are their most well known (Genesis 4:1,2; 5:4). The eldest, Cain, was jealous of his brother Abel so he took him out into the field and slew him (Genesis 4:8). When sin takes over on the inside and we fail to master it, evil is always the external result (Genesis 4:7). Like his parents before him, Cain inherited pain and misery through sin and became a 'restless wanderer' all his days (Genesis 4:11-12).

After Adam and Eve's sin and Cain's act of murder there was good news and bad news in the world. Despite the presence of much sin, something of the creator was still visible in some of his creations. When Seth was born to Abel's parents the Bible records how 'men began to call on the name of the Lord' (Genesis 4:26), and some time later while Adam was still alive, 'Enoch walked with God' so much so that he escaped death (Genesis 5:21-24). 126 years after Adam died Noah was born and he grew up to be 'a righteous man, blameless among the people of his time, and he walked with God' (Genesis 6:9).

Unfortunately these were highlights in a generally depressing slide down to lawlessness and Noah was very much an exception in his day; even his own father killed another man as the level of sin in the world reached catastrophic proportions (Genesis 4:23-24). 'The Lord saw how great man's wickedness on the earth had become, and that every inclination of the thoughts of his heart was only evil all the time. The Lord was grieved that he had made man on the earth, and his heart was filled with pain' (Genesis 6:5-6).

Part of the problem came from the infiltration of more fallen angels who tempted the women sexually (Genesis 6:1-5), but it was the violence which finally stirred God into action (Genesis 6:11-13). The reason he gives for this is very interesting. 'Whoever sheds the blood of man, by man shall his blood be shed; for in the image of God has God made man' (Genesis 9:6). It is not just the human misery and the pain of death and bereavement which God abhors but the destruction of someone made in his image. The Bible considers it first of all a sin *against God* to take away someone else's life unlawfully.

An ark of salvation

Whenever people reject God and his love, his heart is full of pain and yet God never gives up on them. He told Noah to build an ark, to create a place of safety and salvation where people could choose to come and belong. It represents a different kingdom where

God is king and all his subjects are encouraged to love one another as he has first loved us.

St Peter informs us that Noah was 'a preacher of righteousness' (2 Peter 2:5). Maybe he was not a very good preacher, he was certainly not very successful, but at least the people were given the option of salvation. Noah's boat, offering God's love, patience and mercy before judgement came, was there for all to see (1 Peter 3:20).

Jesus said his second coming at the end of the age would be similar to these times. 'As it was in the days of Noah, so it will be at the coming of the Son of Man' (Matthew 24:37).

His teaching was given to remind people of the suddenness of judgement and the need to repent and turn to God before it is too late. His cross, like the ark, is there for all to see.

A rainbow

When the floods came, Noah and his family climbed up the steps into the safe haven created for the purpose but tragically everyone else rejected God's offer of salvation. Only the people who chose to enter the ark were saved along with two of every kind of creature including, presumably, a pair of snakes (Genesis 6:19-20). Judgement is the inevitable consequence of failing to take God up on his offer in the time which is allocated to each of us. Afterwards, when the people who were delivered from death gathered to worship, God made his first covenant with his people and sealed it with the sign of the rainbow (Genesis 9:8-17).

'I establish my covenant with you. Never again will all life be cut off by the waters of a flood; never again will there be a flood to destroy the earth' (Genesis 9:11). Whenever we see a rainbow in the sky after a storm it reminds us of the God who never gives up on us but is always willing to be our God if we will be his people (Jeremiah 24:7; Zechariah 8:8; Revelation 21:3). The covenant was made with Noah but the accruing benefits are available to the whole world. Isaiah foresaw the future glory of Zion as being 'like the days of Noah', refer-ring to the covenant promise after the flood, and looking forward to the day when sin and judgement would be no more (Isaiah 54:9-14).

A ladder

Sadly 'the clans of Noah's sons' who became many nations did not respond to God's love with humility (Genesis 10:32). Apparently, while Noah was still alive, they tried to build a great tower like a ladder reaching into the heavens. This was one ladder in the Bible which became a snake as God came down and confused their speech as a penalty for their arrogance, dividing all the nations of the world from each other.

One day a ladder would come down from heav-en enabling members of every nation to enter heaven; one day the Holy Spirit would be poured out from heaven on all believers, reversing the curse of Babel and enabling them to speak in one another's languages; but until then pride came before a fall. Humankind's own efforts to build a ladder into heaven, to get back into the garden in their own strength, failed at Babel just as they have done ever since. In the Bible, attempts to climb into heaven in our own strength and through our own righteousness are always confounded. It is only when the free gift of God's grace comes down from heaven and people respond to him with thankfulness and humility that access to heaven is granted.

The Church is like the ark

 As in the days of Noah we live in sinful, violent times, but as in the days of Noah there is an ark of salvation available to all who want to live God's way. The Christian Church represents the kingdom of God where people choose freely to become subjects of the king of love. At its best it is a place of love, security, forgiveness and grace; a safe haven in a pernicious and ungodly world.

 Jesus is the head of the Christian Church which bears his name, and is present by his Spirit in every believer. In the same way as Jesus is the image of the Father and made him known when he was on earth in the flesh, so Christians aim to reflect the light of Christ in their midst by his Spirit. No one Christian can be Jesus but *we* are the body of Christ and together we seek to make him known. I have seen him in the lives of many Christians.

During my fifty-plus years in the Christian Church I have been privileged to meet some of the most loving, kind-hearted, generous, unsung people of every denomination up and down the land. Sometimes no one but God notices; sometimes I catch them at it; sometimes it is only the hundreds of cards and flowers at their funerals which tell me of the selfless love they gave to so many in their lifetimes. There are some beautiful Christians in our churches who are worth finding and meeting and all of them are seeking to obey Jesus' commands.

There are basically three main activities which summarise church life. We aim to:

1) Worship God; 2) Love one another; 3) Share the good news of Jesus, all in the power of the Holy Spirit.

1. We come together on Sundays primarily to love and worship God who is the focus of our attention in all our services.

2. He is still the centre of our lives mid-week but in the more informal atmosphere of a housegroup there is greater space and opportunity to care for each other. In the New Testament there are various references to 'loving one another' in many different ways and a quick look at some of them should help us to realise that 'church' based on New Testament principles can never be a Sunday-only activity. (See Appendix 2.)

3. To reach unbelievers with the gospel of Christ we need to be salt and light in the world but when our witness helps friends to become seekers we often require a third church activity which is specially geared to outsiders' needs. Sometimes it is youth groups or over-sixties groups and in recent years discussion groups such as Alpha or Emmaus have proved popular and successful.

During such courses people meet Christians, often feel loved, think through the claims of Christianity in a friendly environment and are encouraged to share doubts and ask questions. Here are some I have been asked.

Is everyone in church weak, wet and wimpish? Many churches have their own 'brown parcel' people; those who live alone, who can only just survive in the community without needing to be institutionalised, who often come to church because it is the only place which welcomes them.

A friend of mine has a son with Down's Syndrome who was not welcome in the local golf club, so he resigned his membership. I'd like to think his son would be welcome in most churches. People come in all shapes and sizes and levels of intellect but I have never met one who became a worse person as a result of becoming a Christian. If you visit a church which is full of 'weak, wet and wimpish' people,

rejoice that they are welcome and God loves them. It probably means you'll be welcome too.

Aren't church members a load of hypocrites? Christians don't
practise what they preach because they preach Jesus, the only
perfect man who ever lived (1 Peter 2:21-22). We do aim to
seek the kingdom of God and his righteousness but sadly we
often fall woefully short of his standards. It is not difficult
catching a Christian committing a sin but hypocrisy is not
something I have encountered much in recent times because
people no longer attend church to be socially acceptable as
they once did. I've often wanted to put up a poster outside
our church which says, 'We're all sinners in here – Come and
join us.' Christians are not perfect, just forgiven.

Hasn't Christianity failed? In the seventies I had an argument with a communist on a street corner who was trying to
sell his magazine. 'You Christians,' he said, 'have had nearly
two thousand years to put the world right, and you failed.
Now it's our turn.'

I didn't give much of an answer at the time but afterwards
I realised the weakness of his point was his presupposition
that Christians are trying to achieve the same thing as
Marxists. The Christian who follows the example of Jesus will
be concerned about social issues, injustice, poverty and the
needs of the world. It is excellent when some feel called into
politics and positions of national leadership to try and impact
the world with Christian love, ethics and beliefs. Even so, the
bigger picture of eternity is the real world for the Christian
and the idea of populating heaven a more realistic goal. We
do not seek to dominate or control the political scene but to
serve a king who washed his disciples' feet (John 13:1-7) and
whose kingdom is not of this world (John 18:36). Moham-
med rode into Mecca on a horse to conquer whereas Jesus
rode into Jerusalem on a donkey to die.

God has not yet removed all sin from the world
because, as in the days of Noah, he is giving unbelievers time to repent (2 Peter 3:9). He never *makes*

anyone a Christian but goes on asking Christians to go on putting the options of his salvation before potential disciples until judgement comes.

The Christian ark is growing

In the world the news seems to be getting worse
and worse but at the same time, in the Church, the good news is getting better and better as those who have eyes to see are becoming more and more aware of the Christian ark which is available today. If I had spoken to the communist a decade or two later we might well have had a different conversation.

The 1980s and 1990s have been the greatest decades of Christian evangelism in the history of humankind. Hundreds of millions have turned to Christ from all over the world as revivals in Africa, China and Latin America are proving contagious.

People are quick to say this is only happening in the rest of the world and not in Britain, but during the same two decades, a tenth of Britain's entire prison population has come to Christ (5,000); a fifth of the gypsy community have been 'born again' (20,000); the Alpha course introducing people to the gospel has reached a million people world wide, and 650,000 so far in the UK; a church in London has grown from 500 to 5,000 in five years and 70,000 people attended renewal meetings in Westminster in 1998. Many of the Church of England theological colleges which faced closure are now overflowing.

America is also important if revival is not to be seen as merely a Third-World phenomenon. In 1991 Dr David Yonggi Cho from South Korea heard God saying, 'I am going to send revival to the seaside city of Pensacola' and this was made public. Since Father's Day 1995, there have already been more conversions to Christ in Brownsville, Pensacola, than in the Welsh revival of 1904 which saw 100,000 people become Christians in a year.

It is my prayer that here in Britain we shall see a significant turning back to God and to the Church so that we can provide a very real alternative society for those who would rather seek God's kingdom and his righteousness, than the one offered by the world. It was finding this alternative Christian society that led Roger Jones to Christ and nurtured him in the faith.

Saved, safe and secure in the ark

 Harold and Winnie were never very keen on church but they permitted Roger to attend a Methodist Sunday school where he met a piano teacher who gave him lessons. Later, as part of his musical education, he began playing the organ for St Paul's Anglican Church and, at the age of thirteen, he accompanied their sung evensong regularly on a Wednesday night. As a young teenager this was his sole contact with church and although it made little impact on him at the time, Roger did know of its existence.

The change came when he entered the sixth form at Saltley Grammar School and began dating Margaret, the deputy head girl. Margaret was a nominal Anglican but introduced him to the Christian Endeavour meetings held at Grenfell Baptist Church on Friday nights. In those days entertainment was limited and quite expensive, a trip to the cinema was a rare treat, so Roger found his regular social life in the Friday night gatherings.

The people at Grenfell were warm, welcoming and loving and seemed genuinely interested in Roger as a person rather than simply using his musical talents. The leaders and the friends he met were far from weak, wet and wimpish and the abundance of attractive females who were present every Friday made it far from boring. No one suggested that turning to Jesus would solve every problem overnight nor that in a few years they would collectively put the world right but testimonies regularly pointed to the difference Jesus can make. Real problems were met head-on with realistic discussion while the claims of Christ were presented interestingly without pulling any punches.

These were enjoyable evenings with plenty of fun and friendship but their serious side also stretched those who attended. Important truths were learnt and repeated which may have proved a bit too much for Roger had he not switched his romantic allegiance from Margaret to Joy. He found himself exchanging a nominal Anglican for a red-hot Baptist and now needed to concentrate on his spiritual lessons in order to stay in favour. This also meant delivering handbills and persuading people to come to a Billy Graham film.

Billy spoke from Psalm 8 with pictures of the solar system in the background. 'When I consider your heavens, the work of your fingers, the moon and the stars, which you have set in place, what is man that you are mindful of him?' (Psalm 8:3-4). The phrase 'what is man?' kept recurring in Roger's mind until he realised the greatness of God, the smallness of Roger and his own need for salvation. At the point of challenge Roger said, 'yes', in his mind and though he didn't go forward it was an informed 'yes'. By now he'd met the alternative society, seen some of their lives, read quite a lot of Scripture and knew something of the cost.

As a natural consequence of all that led up to this moment Roger asked Jesus to be his Lord and Saviour in the privacy of his own room and wrote to Joy telling her what he'd done. She wrote to her minister who met with Roger and it was not long before he was undergoing total immersion baptism at which he gave his testimony. He was eighteen at the time.

After he'd completed 'A' levels Roger left school to attend the Birmingham School of Music where he met a Christian called Steve who helped to nurture him and establish him in the faith. Between them they started a Christian Union and before Roger had been a Christian twelve months he'd been involved in leading nine people to Christ. So successful was the CU that eventually the college principal limited them to only one meeting a day. As Steve had been a Christian for some time Roger learnt a lot from him, and together, with God's help, a Christian society was built up in a small college where everyone had the opportunity of seeing and hearing the good news of Jesus. It was also a society which helped Roger to build the rest of his life on the foundation of Christ.

As in the days of Noah we live in a world tainted by corruption and violence but it doesn't have to be that way for all of us. There is an alternative society, like the ark, which seeks first the kingdom of God and his righteousness where all are welcome. It is a place where our aim is to love God and to love one another as he has first loved us. I'd much rather sit on a hard wooden pew in church than in the law courts.

GROUP STUDY *The Church*

A teasing question: Two men lived and never died, one man lived and never lied and the oldest man who ever lived died before his father. Can you identify them?

Read John 17:20-26.

1. For whom is Jesus praying? (John 17:20).
2. How may the world know that God sent Jesus? (John 17:21,23).
3. How may the world know that God loves Jesus and the Church? (John 17:23,26).
4. How may we help Jesus' prayers to be answered? How do you think we are doing? How may we do better? (John 17:21,23,24).
5. What does Jesus want us to see? (John 17:24).
6. What are the most important things in church life according to Jesus?
7. How may we know Jesus and make him known?

5 A STAIRWAY TO HEAVEN

Father Abraham and sons

The man in the car park looked menacing. If he hadn't been waving his arms frantically and moving around frenetically I might have thought he was hewn out of granite, so strong were his features. He was big, hairy, scruffily dressed in ancient tatters and those he approached could have been forgiven for thinking he'd spent the night in a swamp. Moving among the Rolls Royces, Mercedes and Jaguars beside the club house of the exclusive Wentworth Golf Club he stood out like a sore tower-block.

As the man drew near to us waving madly, my dad interpreted his gesticulations correctly and parked our modest Morris neatly in the appropriate space. Before we took our clubs out of the car, father made a point of approaching him and chatting to him like a long-lost friend. My dad was like that and always treated everybody in the same friendly manner.

When we arrived in the men's locker room there were a few famous faces around and dad quite naturally chatted to the nearest one in exactly the same way as he'd spoken to Swampy. As we made our way to the first tee I asked him if he realised he'd been speaking to Danny Blanchflower, the former Spurs and Northern Ireland football captain. 'Of course,' he replied, 'but he's no different from any of us. I always try to speak to everyone I meet in the same way.'

In 1975 my father and I went to Israel together. I was a theological student and the college authorities graciously allowed my parents to come with a group of future vicars on a two-week lecture-study trip. My parents were never ones for showing much emotion but I shall never forget their reaction when our coach arrived in Jerusalem. They looked lovingly into each other's eyes as dad squeezed mum's hand. I hadn't realised it when we booked the tour but visiting the holy city was one of the main reasons why they'd come. My dad was a captain in the Royal Engineers during the war and wrote a number of letters home from there. They were married in 1940 then didn't see each other for five years. My mum had never been to Israel before and it meant a lot to her.

While we were staying in Jerusalem, father did three things which took me completely by surprise. First, he tried to find all the cricket pitches in Jerusalem where he'd batted. Sadly, cricket didn't seem to have the same priority for modern Israel as it had done for the British Army and we couldn't find the archaeological remains of any wickets, outfields, scoreboards or pavilions.

Secondly, dad rose early every morning for a week to

attend optional morning prayers at Christ Church beside the Jaffa Gate. There were only two or three others who attended regularly, so naturally my father was asked to lead the prayers at one of the sessions. Little did the lecturer who asked him know that my dad had never done anything like this before in his life. I even leapt out of bed early myself that morning to witness it and support him.

'Psalm 122,' he began, 'verse 6. Pray for the peace of Jerusalem: "May those who love you be secure. May there be peace within your walls and security within your citadels"' (Psalm 122:6-7). He then led prayers for Jerusalem, the nation of Israel and peace in the Middle East quite beautifully. We never talked about it but having fought for five years against those who murdered six million Jews, and lived in Palestine for some of that time, it meant enough for him to rise early every morning while in Jerusalem, lead a prayer session for the first time in his life, and to pray for the Jews.

My third great surprise came when our bus took us out into the hills to see some of the countryside. We stopped for a twenty-minute break to rest and take photographs and almost before the doors were opened my dad disappeared. No one saw where he went and we were quite concerned until eventually he was spotted making his way alone towards some Bedouin tents several hundred yards away. 'He ought not to be doing that,' said our guide. 'The Arabs are not always friendly towards those who travel in Jewish coaches.'

I looked in a puzzled way towards my mum. 'I think he wants to try out his Arabic,' she said. We fixed our eyes on the horizon and eventually observed him disappearing into one of the tents. My mother didn't seem as perturbed as the rest of us but after fifteen minutes when the guide said it was almost time to go, and dad hadn't re-appeared, even she began to look a little concerned. We worried needlessly, however, because right on cue he emerged laden with large bunches of grapes and water melons. There were great scenes of hugging and 'humdillallahing' outside the tent before he returned in triumph like Caleb and Joshua carrying fruit back from the promised land. The Arabs had been delighted to see him and when he spoke to them in their own native tongue had welcomed him among them with typical middle-eastern hospitality.

My father always treated everyone the same: poor and rich; Catholics and Protestants; blacks and whites; Arabs and Jews; and I loved him for it.

God's covenant with Abraham

Abraham was fifty-eight years old when Noah died by which time the pattern for God's relationship with his people was beginning to unfold. God loved Adam and Eve and promised to pour untold blessings upon them and their descendants (Genesis 1:27-31). He loved Noah and his family, saved them, protected them and promised worldwide blessings on them and all who come after them (Genesis 9:7-11). A similar picture now emerges with Abraham.

'The Lord said to Abram, "Leave your country, your people and your father's household and go to the land I will show you. I will make you into a great nation and I will bless you;. . .all peoples on earth will be blessed through you"' (Genesis 12:1-3).

It is blessings all the way for Adam, Noah and Abraham – and through them blessings all the way for 'all peoples on earth'. It is only when sinful people spoil the blessings that God's judgement comes into play.

The blessings of the garden of Eden cannot be ruined by sin, so Adam and Eve and Satan were removed from it just as Satan had been removed from heaven before that. Most of the people in Noah's time were perverting and tainting the world so they were removed from the world. It is like the naughty child in a school classroom who prevents the others from learning and is sent out. It is the consequence of sin. In Abraham's time the people of Sodom and Gomorrah were the snakes in the grass who were removed.

But the purposes of God are blessings. This can be seen in the four basic promises God made in his covenant agreement with Abraham; the father of the Jews who was born and brought up in Iraq.

1. As for me, this is my covenant with you: You will be the father of *many nations*. No longer will you be called Abram; your name will be Abraham, for I have made you a father of *many nations* (Genesis 17:4-5).
2. I will establish my covenant as an everlasting covenant between me and you and your descendants after you for the generations to come, to be your God and the *God of your descendants* after you (Genesis 17:7).
3. The whole *land of Canaan*, where you are now an alien, I will give as an everlasting possession to you and your descendants after you (Genesis 17:8).
4. *All peoples on earth* will be blessed through you (Genesis 12:3; 22:18).

It is important to note that the blessings are intended for 'all peoples on earth'. The great nation of Israel which Abraham fathers will be blessed with the land of Canaan but only as part of the whole package of blessings intended for everyone. The 'chosen people' of Israel were chosen for the purpose of bringing the blessings of God to 'all peoples', as we shall see later. The rest of the book of Genesis sees the beginning of God's promises being fulfilled. He started with children.

Isaac

God promised Abram, 'a son coming from your own body will be your heir' (Genesis 15:4). God's plan for fulfilling his own prophecy is revealed when three 'men' visit Abraham and Sarah. They were told Sarah would have a son in a year's time, despite being 'past the age of childbearing' (Genesis 18:11).

 Two of the visitors left for Sodom and were called 'angels' (Genesis 19:1), but the third stayed to talk with Abraham and was called 'the Lord' (Genesis 18:17,20, 26, 33). Abraham pleaded with him for mercy for Sodom and Gomorrah because his nephew Lot was there. The Lord 'remembered Abraham and brought Lot out of the catastrophe' but destroyed Sodom and Gomorrah because their sin was 'so grievous' (Genesis 18:20;19:29). The good work of Noah and the purging of the land through the flood had only brought limited benefits to the world as evil continued to flourish. Snakes had obviously survived the deluge.

 Once more it was necessary for God to take drastic action in dealing with serious sin. Who was this 'man' called 'the Lord' whom Abraham treated as God in his intercessions? A second Christophany is possible: this, too, may have been Jesus walking unnamed through the pages of the Old Testament.

As expected, Sarah gave birth to Isaac a year later but when he was a few years old God hit them with a bombshell. 'Then God said, "Take your son, your only son, Isaac, whom you love, and go to the region of Moriah. Sacrifice him there as a burnt offering on one of the mountains I will tell you about"' (Genesis 22:2).

God tested Abraham by asking him to kill Isaac and sacrifice him on an altar at Mount Moriah. This is often thought to be Mount Zion where Jerusalem was built later and where God sacrificed his own Son for the sins of the whole world. Sometimes God's promises are accompanied by his request for a sacrifice.

Christians in Britain are not normally asked by God to sacrifice their children literally, but the principle of being willing to give up everything for God is a challenge the Lord sometimes puts before us.

Father Roger has many sons

Roger Jones has three sons, Tim, Andrew and Peter, born in 1975, 1977 and 1979 respectively. His wife Mary suffered post-natal depression with all three but after that they proved to be great blessings.

In early 1981 Mary discovered she was pregnant again and thought God said to her, 'You will have a daughter.' After three splendid boys Mary thought a daughter would be quite nice, so she said, 'yes,' to God and told Roger about it. Tim's favourite book at the time was about two hedgehogs with a baby called Sally, a derivative of Sarah, consequently the new baby was only ever going to be called 'Sally'.

Mary began to prepare for the birth of a girl but by March 'Sally' was fighting for her life. Mary took to her bed and began questioning God about what he was doing even though she still accepted the word to her as from him. Later that month Mary miscarried at four and a half months, dealing with it all herself as a qualified nurse who'd previously helped others in this situation. She remembers looking at the tiny dead baby in the palm of her hand with his hands covering his eyes. Later they named him Ian.

In the summer of 1982 Roger and Mary visited Whatcomb House in Dorset, for a summer holiday with the East Birmingham Renewal Group which included my wife Carol and me. During an evening worship session Mary was sitting at the back with Roger at the front while Eric Sellgren led the proceedings. Without knowing anything about their situation he shared a 'word' which he thought he'd received from God. 'There may be a couple here,' he began, 'who've lost a baby. I'm seeing the child in heaven growing up and the parents coming to him, meeting him and recognising him.'

Independently Roger and Mary were both released into tears as they grieved for the death of Ian and the unfulfilled word. Others comforted them and they experienced a deep inner healing. God is very good even when we don't fully understand his ways.

Later that year, now thirty-eight, Mary became pregnant again. In the East Birmingham Renewal Group we were all very concerned. What if? When is a 'word' from God and when is it our own wishful thinking? We prayed much that winter.

At the time Roger's musical about Pentecost, *Saints Alive*, had been recently published and was doing well and he'd already accepted an invitation to perform it with an adult choir in Israel during the summer half-term, leaving on 29 May 1983. The baby was due on 18 May.

In January and February Roger spoke confidently about how God would work out the dates and he sounded very spiritual and holy. By April he was saying the same things but not so loudly. In May, particularly when the 18th came and went without a murmur, he was positively panicking. 'What are you playing at God?' he enquired, before, during and after his daily quiet time. 'Whose musical is this?' Good question but the answer never came.

The first three boys had been born late and once more Mary refused an induction. Roger was angry with God, angry with Mary and angry with himself for being angry. The time for the sacrifice had come.

'Would Mary be happy with another delightful little boy?'

Well . . . er . . . yes. Of course.

All life is a gift from God.

'Would Roger hand over his baton to someone else?'

Well . . . er . . . yes. Of course.

Only God is indispensable.

Roger and Mary can recall the details of 28 May 1983, very well. Sister-in-law Sheila was there to help with Mary and the children when good friend and good musician Martin was invited to the house. Ceremonially, in front of witnesses, Roger took his baton and musical score and handed it over to Martin who received it graciously. Father Roger needed to be at home with Mary.

Mary's waters broke soon after that – during fish and chips at lunch-time. At 8.30pm Mary gave birth to a healthy baby. Roger was there and they called her Sally.

'It's all right,' said Sally's mum sitting up and cradling the new baby in her arms. 'You can go now.'

In the end Roger did not have to sacrifice baton or baby and neither did Abraham have to sacrifice Isaac. An angel stopped Abraham at the last moment and a ram caught in a thicket was substituted for Isaac, but Abraham's obedience, like Jesus' obedience on the cross, continued to bring the promise of universal benefits.

'"I swear by myself," declares the Lord, "that because you have done this and have not withheld your son, your only son . . . *all nations* on earth will be blessed, because you have obeyed me"' (Genesis 22:16-18).

Now that Abraham and Sarah had a son God's covenant promises could be fulfilled.

Jacob's ladder

Isaac married Rebekah who produced twins and God confirmed the covenant he made with Abraham and Isaac to Jacob, the younger, in a dream. A ladder appeared linking heaven to earth with 'angels of God . . . ascending and descending on it' (Genesis 28:12). Unlike the Tower of Babel this one came from God. The Lord said:

I am the Lord, the God of your father Abraham and the God of Isaac. I will give you and your descendants the land on which you are lying. Your descendants will be like the dust of the earth, and you will spread out to the west and to the east, to the north and to the south. *All peoples* on earth will be blessed through you and your offspring.

(Genesis 28:13-14)

The land of Canaan will be given by God to Jacob and his descendants and the universal blessing which will come through them is confirmed. Later Jacob wrestled with God and received the name of the nation he would father. 'A man wrestled with him till day-break', and then said, 'Your name will no longer be Jacob, but Israel because you have struggled with God . . . Then he blessed him there' (Genesis 32:24-30). Jacob limped for the rest of his days but was convinced he saw 'God face to face' (Genesis 32:30). This is yet another appearance of a man called 'God' providing us with possible Christophany number three. It is rather fun seeing Jesus as an all-in-wrestler.

By the end of Genesis parts of the covenant are up and running. The descendants of Abraham, who had six more sons by a second wife after Sarah's death, have become several nations (Genesis 25:1-3). God has been with Abraham, Isaac, Jacob and Joseph who have all kept their side of the covenant which God insisted must be kept (Genesis 17:9-10,14). Joseph has been a great blessing to Egypt and surrounding nations but the nation of Israel and the land of Canaan are yet to come. Blessings for 'all peoples' through Abraham's family only arrive many years later through Jesus.

Jesus brings blessings for everyone

 Before Jesus is born, first Mary and then Zechariah prophesy, linking Jesus to God's covenant promises to Abraham (Luke 1:54-55; 1:67-75). Similarly

Simeon then says this as he sees baby Jesus: 'My eyes have seen your salvation, which you have prepared in the sight of *all people*, a light for revelation to the Gentiles and for glory to your people Israel' (Luke 2:30-32).

'All people', Gentiles and Jews, will be blessed by this Messiah. Through the line of Father Abraham comes Jesus (Matthew 1:1) offering eternal salvation to everyone from all nations. 'For God so loved the world that he gave his one and only Son, that *whoever* believes in him shall not perish but have eternal life' (John 3:16). *Whoever* believes, receives. Heavenly blessings can come through Jesus to all nations of the world because he is the ladder who comes down from heaven to the earth.

Jesus is the ladder from heaven

Jesus sees himself, the Son of Man, as the New Testament version of Jacob's ladder connecting heaven and earth. 'Jesus said, "I tell you the truth, you shall see heaven open, and the angels of God ascending and descending on the Son of Man"' (John 1:51).

Jacob described the place where he saw the ladder touch the earth as 'the gate of heaven' (Genesis 28:17) and Jesus said, 'I am the gate; whoever enters through me will be saved' (John 10:9). Jacob saw the Lord standing above the ladder, in heaven (Genesis 28:13), and Jesus said, 'I am the the way and the truth and the life. No-one comes to the Father except through me' (John 14:6). God said to Jacob, 'All peoples on earth will be blessed through you and your offspring' (Genesis 28:14) and Jesus, Jacob's descendant, said, 'Whoever lives and believes in me will never die' (John 11:26). Blessings indeed for eveyone from all nations who accept Christ.

The responsibility for spreading this wonderful news to *all nations* was given to the first disciples who were all Jews

(Matthew 28:18-20). St Peter received God's message, up a ladder on a roof, becoming the first one to take the gospel of Jesus Christ to the non-Jews, and when he saw God's Holy Spirit coming on them he responded warmly. 'I now realise how true it is that God does not show favouritism,' he said, 'but accepts men from every nation who fear him and do what is right' (Acts 10:34-35).

St Paul was known as the Apostle to the Gentiles and when he wrote to Jewish Christians in Galatia he reminded them of the equal status for all who have accepted Jesus as the Messiah. Having argued that 'those who believe are children of Abraham' (Galatians 3:7) he then continued: 'There is neither Jew nor Greek, slave nor free, male nor female, for you are all one in Christ Jesus. If you belong to Christ, then you are *Abraham's* seed, and heirs according to the promise' (Galatians 3:28-29).

God's promise to Abraham that all peoples on earth will be blessed through him comes to fruition in Jesus, the son of Abraham (Matthew 1:1). Those who accept Jesus as the Christ, God's Messiah, whether Jew or Gentile, become children of God, enter God's kingdom, and receive the free gift of eternal life.

All one in Christ Jesus

The trip to Israel went well and Roger now takes adult choirs regularly to Jerusalem. Half of the party normally stay at Christ Church in the Jewish sector of the Old City and the other half stay in East Jerusalem at St George's Cathedral. Christ Church has two Hebrew congregations attached to it and has the Ten Commandments and the Lord's Prayer written in Hebrew on the wall. St George's has *Hymns Ancient and Modern* and the *Book of Common Prayer* available in Arabic, but the worship of Jesus seems to unite them. People come from Christ

Church to help in the musicals at St George's and vice versa and at many of Roger's productions Jews and Arabs are worshipping God together in the same congregation.

If we ask any child in Sunday school, 'Does God love boys more than girls, rich more than poor, whites more than blacks, Jews more than Arabs?' they will nearly always answer, 'Of course not. He loves everyone the same.' In Christ Jesus all nations can be blessed for with God there is no favouritism (Acts 10:34; Romans 2:11; Ephesians 6:9; Colossians 3:25; 1 Timothy 5:21). In the alternative society of the Christian Church it is wonderful to realise that all believers, young and old, fat and thin, bright or not so bright, from whatever class, country or culture they come, are all one in Christ Jesus, and all receive the blessings promised to Abraham (Galatians 3:28-29). It is a kingdom without apartheid where the king loves everyone equally and keeps his promises to those who love him for ever.

GROUP STUDY *All one in Christ*

A daily question: What is God's favourite day of the week?

Read John 4:1-14.

1. Why did John mention that land owned by Jacob and Joseph was in Samaria? (John 4:4-6).
2. Why do you think he records that Jesus was tired? (John 4:6). What does this sort of detail tell us about the author?
3. Why was the Samaritan woman surprised when Jesus asked her for a drink? (John 4:9). Did Jesus ever get his drink?
4. What was Jesus saying by asking a Samaritan woman for a drink? What 'people-groups' might suffer most from our

prejudices? How can we avoid it happenning and be more like Jesus?

5. Who can help us? (John 4:10). What is the living water to which Jesus referred? (John 7:37-39).

6. How may we receive living water? (John 4:10-14).

7. Is Jesus greater than Father Jacob? (John 4:12). In what ways?

6 A SNAKE BECOMES A LADDER

Just as Moses

One Saturday morning I was working in my study when I began to feel strangely warmed. Immediately I stopped what I was doing, went over to an armchair, sat down, closed my eyes and waited for God to speak to me. It felt like an involuntary action as something indefinable stirred in my spirit.

I prayed, 'Come Holy Spirit,' after which I found my thoughts turning to Roger Jones who was ministering in another church that weekend. An interesting message formed in my mind. 'Tell Roger to give out this "word" at the Sunday-evening service. There will be a teenage girl present with a pain in the lower part of the neck near her shoulder.' And then a further instruction. 'Tell the person who sees her that the pain in the neck is not the main reason I want her to come forward.'

Although it was not I who would look a fool at the church service, I didn't much fancy the idea of being wrong. How could I know if it was right? What test could be applied? All I seemed to have was my own inner turmoil and struggle but maybe that in itself was saying something?

I phoned my message through to Mary Jones who relayed it to her husband late on Saturday night. In recent years Roger has been faithful in sharing possible 'words' from God which praying supporters have given him even though he is often invited to speak in churches of differing spiritual shades and churchmanships. During this time more people have been saved, healed and delivered than previously and more letters of criticism have been sent to him. It is a costly ministry. Roger risked it and gave it out at the Sunday-evening service along with several other 'words' which he and the team received.

Two teenage girls attended all the meetings over the weekend. One of them was a committed Christian worshipping regularly in the church while the other was a friend she'd invited. At the very first session Roger's talk gave the friend a pain in the neck. It was a genuine, physical pain which stayed with her all weekend, and she told her friend about it.

When Roger gave the 'word' on Sunday evening, the Christian girl nudged her friend. 'That's for you,' she said. The friend nodded and agreed to go with her to the front. As soon as she left her chair the pain in the neck also left, never to return, but the girls still came forward.

Gill, a member of Roger's team, was waiting for them. Roger gave Gill the further instruction enabling her to be ready with a few sensitive questions. 'Yes', one was definitely a committed Christian but 'no', her friend was not.

Encouraged by all she'd heard about Jesus and experienced during the weekend, especially the 'word' and the physical sign in her neck, the friend confessed her new belief and accepted Jesus Christ as her personal Saviour. Her buddy promised to help nurture her in the Christian faith.

The teenage girl experienced a sign of God's presence when Roger gave a 'word' about her neck and it helped her to believe in God's love for her personally. She then entered into a covenant relationship with God as she committed her life to Christ. Signs and wonders can be very helpful in encouraging people to believe and they can be seen throughout the story of deliverance from Egypt (Exodus 3-14).

The Exodus

The Old Testament account of the Exodus contains the one covenant relationship with God which is *not* about new promises and blessings. It is about the fulfilment of God's old covenant promises made to Abraham. Here is the task God set himself if he was to keep his word to Abraham, Isaac, Jacob and sons, the Patriarchs:

1. To take a family of wandering bedouins, who lived off the land and kept sheep, and turn them into a great nation.
2. To convince them of God's love, mercy and justice so that they willingly entered into a covenant relationship with him.
3. To give them a land where others already lived.
4. To enable them to bring blessings to all peoples on earth.

This is how God did it without ever compromising his own holiness and righteousness yet accomplishing his purposes and promises by allowing for the good and evil in people.

Gathering together

 God began by bringing the wandering, far-flung extended family of Jacob together in one place. He took Joseph, Jacob's eleventh son but his first by Rachel, and used the dreamer's conceit coupled with his dad's favouritism to obtain a free trip to Egypt. Poverty and starvation caused Jacob and the rest of the family to join Joseph in Egypt where the boredom and oppression of subsequent slavery encouraged them to breed like rabbits (Acts 7:17).

We now have plenty of people, all descended from the Patriarchs, in one location.

A common goal

Lack of unity is a big problem facing anyone who desires to create a great nation. In the time of Joseph, who became Egypt's vizier, or prime minister, life was relaxed and prosperous (Genesis 41:41). They weren't in their own land, they weren't a great nation but who cared as long as they were comfortable? Their eventual bondage and harsh treatment from Pharaoh, King of Egypt, after Joseph had died, united them in their calling out to God and gave them a common goal in their cry for freedom.

Prince of Egypt

Where does a powerless, downtrodden band of slaves find an educated, skilled, equipped leader who will be willing to plead their cause? Ironically as Pharaoh decided to murder all the Hebrew baby boys because of over-population he set up an opportunity for the Israelite Moses, via a basket in the bulrushes, to be schooled for leadership in the palace. The king's daughter found baby Moses in the bulrushes, adopted him and gave him the best education available in the civilised world at the time. Moses still saw the Hebrews as 'his own people' and identified with them, consequently a trained leader with Israelite roots and sympathies became equipped for action. After several hundred years many people were gathered together, united in purpose, with one of their number ready to become their shepherd; all they lacked now was the power (Exodus 2:11).

Signs and wonders

'So Moses thought; I will go over and see this strange sight – why the bush does not burn up' (Exodus 3:3).

Moses went to see a burning bush and found the living God waiting for him with a job description in two parts.
1. Free the Israelites to worship God in the desert.
2. Lead them to the Promised Land.

The power of God for beginning the task was found to be in Moses' own hands.

Then the Lord said to him, 'What is that in your hand?' 'A staff,' he replied. The Lord said, 'Throw it on the ground.' Moses threw it on the ground and it became a snake, and he ran from it. Then the Lord said to him, 'Reach out your hand and take it by the tail.' So Moses reached out and took hold of the snake and it turned back into a staff in his hand.

(Exodus 4:2-4)

A pole and a snake in the hands of the living God became like a ladder giving Moses a leg up to get him going. God called it a 'miraculous sign'; a pointer to the presence and power of God and his love for his people (Exodus 4:8). It was but one of many signs that were necessary before Egypt released them.

Moses' brother Aaron took 'the staff that was changed

into a snake' in his hand and struck the Nile which turned into blood, and later used it to bring plagues of frogs and gnats on the Egyptians (Exodus 7:15 - 8:19). Pharaoh and his people suffered one plague after another but there were no flies on Moses. Finally God said, 'I will *pass over* you. You must slaughter a lamb in each household and put some of its blood on the door-frames of the houses where you eat the roasted meat.'

 As God came in the night the obedient Hebrews were spared but the firstborn male in every Egyptian family died. God punished them for murdering the Israelite babies and in so doing released his people as Pharaoh in his grief then let them go.

After they had been led by pillars of cloud and fire, guided through the parting waters of the Red Sea and fed by manna in the desert, the time arrived for God's third covenant with his people. God's signs and wonders had encouraged them to believe and now they were ready to consider his offer favourably.

The covenant

The new nation with its own prince chose to become God's people in the desert. On Mount Sinai God's presence in thick cloud was gloriously announced with thunder, lightning and 'a very loud trumpet blast' (Exodus 19:16). With his finger God wrote the Ten Commandments on two tablets of stone summarising what he required from his people if he was to be their God. They agreed to his terms and the covenant was sealed with blood. 'Moses then took the blood, sprinkled it on the people and said, "This is the blood of the covenant that the Lord has made with you in accordance with all these words"' (Exodus 24:8).

 Unfortunately the Exodus story from Mount Sinai onwards was one of disobedience and lack of trust in God which led to a forty-year sandy slog in the wilderness until all the unbelievers had died. Years later, after Aaron's death, Yahweh used his power over snakes once more to help his unfaithful people to believe in him. ' "Why have you brought us up out of Egypt," they asked, "to die in the desert? There is no bread! There is no water! And we detest this miserable food." Then the Lord sent venomous snakes among them; they bit the people and many Israelites died' (Numbers 21:5-6).

'The people came to Moses and said, "We sinned when we spoke against the Lord and against you. Pray that the Lord will take the snakes away from us." So Moses prayed for the people' (Numbers 21:7).

Just as with the blood of the lamb on the doorposts, God offered healing linked to a visible sign: 'The Lord said to Moses, "Make a snake and put it up on a pole; anyone who is bitten can look at it and live." So Moses made a bronze snake and put it up on a pole. Then when anyone was bitten by a snake and looked at the bronze snake, he lived' (Numbers 21:8-9).

This time the pole and the snake came together as a sign becoming like a ladder to God's wholeness. Those who expressed obedience and faith in God by looking up at the snake in pole position were healed. Thus, with consistent use of signs and wonders, God demonstrated his power over Satan, the serpent, evil, oppression and now sickness.

The signs of God's presence in the Exodus story encouraged the people to believe and to know the God of Abraham, Isaac and Jacob for themselves in a new covenant relationship. They had become a nation, God's people, and were on their way towards the land flowing with milk and honey promised to Abraham.

The Promised Land

When God made the covenant vow to Abram regarding the land, while he was in a deep, dark sleep, he informed him his descendants would return from slavery in a 'country not their own' and punish Canaan's inhabitants for their sins (Genesis 15:12-16). God told Moses the people of Canaan had sinned against him by involving themselves in all kinds of sexual immorality, idolatry and sacrificing children to Molech (Leviticus 18-20). So, after Moses' death, when Joshua, the new leader, was commissioned to possess the land, he was also required by God to bring judgement on certain cities, such as Jericho. It was similar to the flood in Noah's day, the fire which came down from heaven on Sodom and Gomorrah, and the Passover plague of death which judged the baby-killing Egyptians, only this time it was done with the sword. Rahab and her family from Jericho were spared because they were kind to the Israelite spies but everyone else in the city perished. It is interesting to note who helped Joshua to win the battle.

A man came to him with a drawn sword claiming to have come 'as commander of the army of the Lord' (Joshua 5:14). When Joshua fell face down in reverence the commander said, 'Take off your sandals, for the place where you are standing is holy' (Joshua 5:15). The similarity between this and the appearance of Yahweh to Moses at the burning bush has led some to suggest another Christophany. After this encounter, Joshua is assisted by the Lord in conquering the territory promised to Israel.

By the end of the book of Joshua God has taken a family of wandering bedouins and made them into a powerful nation. He has convinced them of his love, mercy and justice with signs and wonders and they have responded by willingly entering into a covenant relationship with him. The people of Israel are now occupying the land of Canaan, and only the blessings for 'all peoples' are yet to be accomplished from all the promises God made to Abraham. This was achieved with a new covenant.

Jesus

'Just as Moses lifted up the snake in the desert so the Son of Man must be lifted up that every one who believes in him may have eternal life' (John 3:14-15).

Those who look at Jesus on the cross, see and believe, escape from spiritual death and receive eternal life. They enter the new covenant with God, sealed by the blood of Christ. On the night he was arrested Jesus said, 'This cup is the new covenant in my blood, which is poured out for you' (Luke 22:20). Many times the 'Exodus motif' is used by the writers of the New Testament to show how the new covenant God offers to us through Jesus is like the one made to Moses but better in every way (see Appendix 3). It is a covenant which fulfils God's promises to the Patriarchs in an eternal unseen spiritual realm which nobody could ever have imagined. Anyone and everyone from all nations who believe in Jesus become God's children and the miracles he does among us help us to believe.

Signs of God's presence

The Israelites believed in the invisible Yahweh and entered into a covenant with him because of the signs and wonders he did in their midst. Just as with Moses and the Old Covenant the pattern is repeated with Jesus and the new one. The unseen kingdom of God was advanced when people like Nathaniel believed in Jesus because of a sign (John 1:48-50). John also records that Jesus' other disciples put their faith in him when he turned water into wine (John 2:11). Jesus said this to those who had difficulty believing in him: 'Believe me when I say that I am in the Father and the Father is in me; or at least believe on the evidence of the miracles themselves' (John 14:11).

The resurrection of Jesus from the dead was the most important sign of God's presence, power and love given to Jesus' followers and this enabled them to believe in Jesus and his sacrificial death. Anyone can promise life after death but only he who has come through death and returned to confirm his promise is worth believing.

Once the people believed Moses and obeyed God by looking at the snake on the pole, their faith in God was confirmed by the gift of life as those who looked and believed did not die. Jesus' resurrection is the sign that suggests Jesus has the right to offer eternal life through his death on the cross, and those who do believe have their faith confirmed when they are filled with the Holy Spirit. Today the Holy Spirit is the power of God and the presence of the risen Lord Jesus who, though unseen, helps people to believe and to enter the New Covenant relationship with him.

The power of the Holy Spirit

The power which brought the Hebrew slaves out of Egypt; the power which enabled them to possess the Promised Land; the power which raised Jesus from the dead is available to all Christians through Jesus (Acts 2:38-39).

Jesus is the baptiser in the Holy Spirit (John 1:32-33). Jesus says, 'If anyone is thirsty, let him come to me and drink . . . By this he meant the Spirit whom those who believed in him were later to receive' (John 7:37-39). 'After he rose from the dead Jesus breathed on his disciples and said, "Receive the Holy Spirit"' (John 20:22).

Jesus is the one who makes the Father known to us; Jesus is the one who gives us the Holy Spirit; and Jesus is the one who says the Holy Spirit will be more effective than he was. When the Spirit comes greater things will be done (John 14:12); he will accomplish more teaching (John 14:26); and more will believe (John 14:29). There will be more righteousness (John 16:8); more personal counselling (John 16:7); more pastoral care (John 16:13) and more truth revealed (John 16:13). The believers will receive more power (John 16:23) and more blessing (John 20:29).

What good news and what encouragement to the powerless, underprivileged and needy of today's world who are still in spiritual bondage to Pharaoh! Jesus, who is God, is with us by his Spirit; he is in us. There will be greater things, more teaching, more belief, more believers, more righteousness, more pastoral care, more truth, more power than when Jesus was on earth, and more affirmation and blessing than Thomas the Apostle received if we keep going, believe in Jesus and welcome his Holy Spirit.

This is the gospel of Jesus Christ. He is God. He is with us today by his Spirit; he makes the Father known; we can do all things through him. This is the whole package which Jeremiah prophesied (Jeremiah 31:31-34). This is the New Covenant confirmed with signs that the New Testament informs us is far superior to the one made with Moses (Hebrews 3:3; 8:6). And even more amazing is the biblical truth that just as Moses and the Hebrew slaves saw God do signs and wonders to help them believe; just as the first disciples saw Jesus do signs and wonders which helped them to believe; just as the early Church did signs and wonders in the power of the Holy Spirit to help others believe, so we can do the same. 'Jesus said, "Anyone who has faith in me will do what I have been doing"' (John 14:12).

Church leaders who regularly invite God to send his Holy Spirit among them, through Jesus, often find people are helped to believe in Jesus and enter the new covenant agreement with God by the signs of his presence in their midst.

God with us

Although Roger Jones was well grounded in the Christian faith, his mentor, Steve, was rather anti-charismatic. He was taught that gifts of the Holy Spirit such as speaking in tongues, healing or prophecy died out with the early Church and were not meant

for today. While Roger was at music college in the centre of Birmingham, Tom Walker was on the staff of Birmingham Cathedral, so Roger went along to the lunch-time talks which Tom provided for those who worked or studied in the city.

After one of these Roger spotted Tom's Bible sitting on the edge of the font so he sneaked up to have a look at it. He found 1 Corinthians 12-14 heavily underlined, especially the spiritual gifts, as if they were important and relevant for today. Roger went home, read his own Bible, attended a weekend retreat on the subject and believed. He asked Tom to lay hands on him and pray for him to receive spiritual gifts.

Tom was delighted, placed his hands on Roger's head, asked God to give him the gift of speaking in tongues and spoke in an unknown language over him. Nothing happened. Roger felt nothing, saw nothing and heard nothing, but it was a good 'nothing' because on the way home, by himself, without any feelings of emotion whatsoever, Roger opened his mouth and began to speak out loud in an unknown language. Despite the lack of emotion, deep down inside Roger sensed this was the biblical gift of speaking in tongues and that it was of God.

He returned to tell Tom Walker what had occurred and Tom prayed for him to receive another gift. Shortly afterwards a lady came into the cathedral looking and sounding perfectly normal and Roger said to Tom, 'There's something not quite right about that person.' She saw Tom for counselling and, with permission, he was able to confirm to Roger that she was in fact heavily demonised. The Bible lists this particular gift as 'the discerning of spirits' (1 Corinthians 12:10, KJV).

Receiving and giving 'words' from God is a gift which the Holy Spirit has often brought to Roger. The worst service in my life was the midnight communion on Christmas Eve 1986 when everything went wrong for me until right at the end of the service when Roger walked quietly from the organ stool and spoke gently into the microphone. 'I think God may be saying there is someone here who has been contemplating suicide in this last week. There is a better way; do come and see me.' A man came forward and and said it applied to him and Roger was able to help him know the Lord and not take his own life. The man remained in contact with Roger for a number of years until eventually he went to be with the Lord following a long illness.

At Lee Abbey, (a Christian retreat centre), a lady with arthritis in the leg came to see Roger and Mary requesting prayer, and as they prayed Roger received a prompting inside which said, 'Ask her about family problems.' This opened the floodgates of pain and bitterness until eventually Roger and Mary were able to help the lady to forgive her family. Roger then sensed another prompting to 'curse the arthritis in the name of Jesus' which he did. Later that day the lady appeared without her stick, full of joy, and danced before the Lord; an activity which had been absent from her worship for many months.

On a reasonably regular basis God has used Roger to receive and give 'words' from him and also to encourage others in this ministry. Before a production of, *From Pharaoh to Freedom* in Portsmouth, Roger asked God through Jesus to send his Holy Spirit on the cast. At this point one of them received a sudden twinge in the left-hand side of the jaw, shared it with the conductor, and was relieved to feel it disappear prior to going on stage. Roger mentioned it at the end of the proceedings as a possible 'word' from God and heard nothing more for a week, until a letter arrived at his home. A lady came to the presentation of Pharaoh having nearly committed her life to Christ previously several times. Christian friends were praying for her, loving her, regularly witnessing to her and they brought her to the musical even though she was suffering that night from a raging tooth ache on the left-hand side of her jaw. When Roger gave the 'word' it felt as if God was speaking straight to her and she kept muttering, 'How does he know about me?' The lady became a Christian after the performance when she gladly accepted Jesus as her Lord and Saviour.

 This story is similar to Nathaniel's encounter with Jesus. When the Son of Man said, 'I saw you under the fig tree,' in a land full of fig trees, it was no more specific than a pain in the left-hand side of the jaw, but on both occasions there was enough information to help the person believe in Jesus (John 1:50). Signs from God are not always spectacular and only rarely do they by-pass the normal Christian activities of praying, loving and witnessing, but they often provide a little touch of God's divine presence which helps to seal the deal. The presence, power and signs which come from God through Jesus by his Holy Spirit can help people to believe. The New Testament indicates they are an integral part of mainline Christianity which should be experienced, from time to time, in all churches.

 Just as Moses and Jesus' early disciples witnessed signs of God's presence among them, helping them to enter into a covenant agreement with God, so the New Testament suggests we can do the same.

GROUP STUDY *signs and wonders*

A topical question: How can we look at life through heaven's eyes?

Read John 14:11-21.

1. Why did Jesus' disciples believe in Jesus? (John 14:11).
2. Why did people believe Jesus' disciples? (John 14:12).
3. What do you think Jesus meant by 'greater things than these?' (John 14:12).
   Who can do them? What does 'faith in me' mean?
4. Can we ask Jesus to do *anything* for us? (John 14:13-14). What does 'in my name' suggest to you? Is it related to verses 15 and 21?
5. Who sends the Holy Spirit? (John 14:16,26; 16:7).
6. How do we know the Holy Spirit is a person and not just an impersonal force? (John 14:17).
7. How may we be filled with the Holy Spirit?

7 A TEMPLE WITH STAIRS
King David

It was dark and late when we arrived at our hotel, tired after a long day's travelling, so we went straight to bed. In the morning when my wife Carol drew back the curtains, we found our window filled with a panoramic view of the Old City of Jerusalem, and the burial site of King David closest to us. Panning across to the right, some distance away, we could just make out the Mount of Olives from where Jesus left the earth to return to his Father in heaven.

Carol had never been to Israel before so it was a thrill and a delight to be staying together in the Mount Zion Hotel with such a view from our room, especially as friends were paying for it. I looked forward to taking her to see some of the sites I'd visited with my parents more than twenty years before, but for now it was sufficient simply to look and reflect and read a few scripture verses together. There was certainly something different about staying beside the ancient site where Solomon built the first Temple, Isaiah prophesied and Jesus died. Everything was beautiful as long as we didn't look down into the valley below.

The Valley of Ben Hinnom right beneath us presented itself like a typical modern park or city garden with its green grass and flowering trees but I knew it plastered over one of the most hideous cracks of human history. This was where Manasseh, King of Judah, descendant of David, forefather of Jesus, sacrificed his sons in the fire to Molech (2 Kings 21:6; 23:10; 2 Chronicles 33:6). This was the valley where Judas Iscariot, who betrayed Jesus for thirty pieces of silver, 'hanged himself' (Matthew 27:5) and 'all his intestines spilled out' (Acts 1:18). This is the place pictured at the end of the Bible where 'the dogs, those who practise magic arts, the sexually immoral, the murderers, the idolaters and everyone who loves and practises falsehood' will dwell outside the holy city (Revelation 22:15). This is the valley where they used to burn the offal and all other unclean refuse at a site called 'Gehenna' which in English is normally translated as 'hell'.

Our guides described to us in detail how Manasseh and others burnt their children to death right beneath our hotel window. 'What on earth,' I thought to myself, 'is that king doing in the first chapter of the New Testament which tells us the good news of Jesus Christ?' (Matthew 1:10). 'And why did God wipe out King Saul and all his family but allow Manasseh and his descendants to be the forefathers of the Saviour of the world?'

The first kings of Israel made their appearance about two

hundred and fifty years after Moses. Before then Joshua did well, as did Deborah, Gideon and Samson occasionally, and Samuel was one of the most gifted and anointed prophets of all time. But it was with their second king, David, that God made his fourth covenant. It is clearly stated in Psalm 89. God says: 'I have made a covenant with my chosen one, I have sworn to David my servant, I will establish your line for ever' (Psalm 89:3-4).

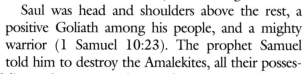

A promise is a promise and when God makes one it always comes to fruition in the fullness of time. But why did he make it with David and not with Saul, the first king of Israel?

Saul was head and shoulders above the rest, a positive Goliath among his people, and a mighty warrior (1 Samuel 10:23). The prophet Samuel told him to destroy the Amalekites, all their possessions and livestock, as a punishment from God. Saul nearly got it right. He killed everyone but the king and all the animals except a few good ones which he kept back to offer as a sacrifice to God. After this God withdrew his Spirit from Saul and the kingship of Israel from his descendants.

David was head and shoulders below the rest of his family when Samuel anointed him to be king in Saul's place, and he looked after the sheep (1 Samuel 16:1-13). King David got it very wrong. He committed voyeurism, adultery and murder and according to God's law, given to Moses, should have been executed, but the Old Testament informs us that David was blessed by God, while Saul was cursed (2 Samuel 7:15-16). In the biblical accounts of David's life we find the reason why God blessed him and forgave him.

King David was a true worshipper of God

David was not as righteous as Noah and he did not always exercise the same faith as Abraham. 'My God, my God,' he cried out in a bad moment, 'why have you forsaken me?'

(Psalm 22:1). At times he discerned the will of God correctly but he was not a prophet like Moses who spoke 'face to face' with God (Numbers 12:8). David became the last person before Christ with whom God made an official covenant, and only the fourth in hundreds of years of history, because he was a true worshipper of God.

David was a shepherd, and it was as he was out on the hills keeping watch over his flocks by night, probably with a harp in his hand, that he found God. 'The heavens declare the glory of God;' he wrote. 'The skies proclaim the work of his hands' (Psalm 19:1). 'The Lord is my shepherd, I shall not want' (Psalm 23:1).

He met God at all times; in the morning (Psalm 5:3), at noon, in the evening (Psalm 55:1,17), all day long (Psalm 25:5), and at night (Psalm 4:8). He found him in all places.

> Where can I go from your Spirit? Where can I flee from your presence? If I go up to the heavens, you are there . . . If I rise on the wings of the dawn, if I settle on the far side of the sea, even there your hand will guide me, your right hand will hold me fast.
>
> (Psalm 139:7-10)

A sense of peace and patience in God's presence emerged from David's times of prayer and meditation. 'I waited patiently for the Lord' (Psalm 40:1) he declared, and 'My soul finds rest in God alone' (Psalm 62:1). All of which led David naturally into worship and praise.

He put a new song in my mouth, a hymn of praise to our God (Psalm 40:3). And yet David's religion was not an escapist clause hidden in the corner of life's tapestry. God went with him and before him as he strode out to meet Goliath. The giant was head and shoulders above everyone when they came face to face but he was only shoulders above them by the time David had cut him down to size.

The king of Israel, assisted by thousands of troops, tried to capture David and exterminate him but he escaped repeatedly like Zorro. The biblical fugitive, however, won through with prayer and God's guidance rather than gymnastic feats and swordplay, and eventually God gave David victory over all his enemies.

So, when the ark of the covenant symbolising God's presence was brought to Jerusalem, David had confidence in God and a personal relationship with him. From his heart of love and devotion towards God he organised a splendid welcome celebration. The sacrifices were the best money could buy; the songs, harps, lyres, tambourines, sistrums and cymbals gave the whole proceedings a touch of class while a congregation of 30,000 was not bad for a bank-holiday. But then tragedy in the eyes of the world struck as David spoilt the whole show.

Wearing nothing more than a linen ephod, (ie not much more than his boxer shorts), His Royal Highness danced before the Lord with all his might. The court officials were embarrassed and didn't like it one bit; the upper-class averted their eyes with disdain and the queen was not amused (2 Samuel 6:20). God, however, saw it differently.

Following this incident, in the very next chapter, the word of the Lord came to the prophet Nathan at night. 'I will establish the throne of his kingdom for ever. I will be his father, and he shall be my son' (2 Samuel 7:13-14). 'For ever' is a very long time and a covenant promise from God like this is worth noting. What David did was very important.

David worshipped God with his whole being. 'I *will* celebrate before the Lord,' he said making a conscious decision with his mind and will to do it (2 Samuel 6:21). He used his body as he danced before the Lord, and his *emotions* as he did it 'with all his might' (2 Samuel 6:5,14).

David worshipped God in *relationship with others*. The

'whole house of Israel' celebrated with various instruments and the 'entire house of Israel' later with shouts and trumpets (2 Samuel 6:5). David was not always a one-man band.

The heart of David which emerged from the dancing incident was one full of praise for God. He displayed the heart of a true worshipper and this is what saved him when sin came crouching at the bedroom door.

Several years later, 'at a time when kings go off to war', David saw a 'very beautiful' married woman taking a bath and lusted after her (2 Samuel 11:1). He committed adultery with her, some would call it rape, and when she became pregnant the king ordered her husband to be killed. He covered his tracks carefully but the God who loved David saw it all.

Once more God spoke to Nathan, only this time he was sent to confront David with his sin. Receiving such a challenge as this always sorts out the men from the boys and the king's immediate response in the face of such difficult, embarrassing and potentially life-threatening truth, was also that of a true worshipper. 'Then David said to Nathan, "I have sinned against the Lord"' (2 Samuel 12:13).

Psalm 51 is the record of David's subsequent prayer to God which many have used since. The first few verses say it all.

> Have mercy on me, O God, according to your unfailing love; according to your great compassion blot out my transgressions. Wash away all my iniquity and cleanse me from my sin. For I know my transgressions, and my sin is always before me. Against you, you only, have I sinned and done what is evil in your sight, so that you are proved right when you speak and justified when you judge.
>
> (Psalm 51:1-4)

It isn't objectively true that David only sinned against God but it is how he felt. He recognised his transgression was primarily against God, the number-one person in his life. The response of confession and repentance when challenged by

God is the one of a true worshipper who has lived a life of prayer and God meets this honesty and humility with forgiveness. Unfortunately Saul reacted to being confronted by his sin in a totally different way.

King Saul made excuses and told lies

In contrast to David, King Saul got his response to sin all wrong. The heart of Saul is revealed in his argument with Samuel over the Amalekites. 'When Samuel reached him, Saul said, "The Lord bless you! I have carried out the Lord's instruction"' (1 Samuel 15:13). This may have satisfied a lesser prophet but Samuel was not easily deceived. '"What then is this bleating of sheep in my ears?" he asked. "What is this lowing of cattle that I hear?"' (1 Samuel 15:14).

Unlike David, Saul immediately went on the defensive and began making excuses but Samuel interrupted him impatiently (1 Samuel 15:15). '"Stop!" Samuel said to Saul. "Let me tell you what the Lord said to me last night"' (1 Samuel 15:16). He then continued, 'Why did you not obey the Lord?' (1 Samuel 15:19). Alas King Saul condemned himself and his family again with his answer. 'But I did obey the Lord,' Saul said (1 Samuel 15:20). From such a deceitful reply there was no going back and the verdict came quickly. 'Rebellion is as the sin of witchcraft,' said Samuel (1 Samuel 15:23. KJV). 'The Lord has torn the kingdom of Israel from you today' (1 Samuel 16:28).

 Saul tried to make excuses and cover up by telling lies but it didn't work with God and it never will. It always leads to God's withdrawal from the scene which in Bible terms is called cursing.

The message of the Bible is consistent. The size or seriousness of the sin doesn't matter. It is what we do with it that counts. Those who are truly sorry and genuinely want to worship God in humility will always find forgiveness from God, no matter what they have done. Looking down on the

Valley of Hinnom we were tempted to ask whether even Manasseh could have found mercy from God if he had repented? I checked him out in the Second Book of Chronicles.

> In his distress he sought the favour of the Lord his God and humbled himself greatly before the God of his fathers. And when he prayed to him, the Lord was moved by his entreaty and listened to his plea; so he brought him back to Jerusalem and to his kingdom. Then Manasseh knew that the Lord is God.
>
> (2 Chronicles 33:12–13)

God's forgiveness of Manasseh reveals the size of his love and compassion for those who truly repent and this gives great hope to us all.

The temple with a stairway

King David always wanted to build a temple for God in Jerusalem as a house of prayer and worship. In it the use of sacrifices would enable believers to take sin seriously, face up to it with true confession and free them to make their requests known to God with clean hands and pure hearts. Musical instruments would be present to accompany David's many psalms in worship thereby adding the potential for praising God with all their might. The people of God considered prayer and praise to be so important that a whole tribe of Levites, one thirteenth of the nation of Israel, was set aside to oversee both activities as well as the necessary sacrifices.

In the end David was only allowed to order the stones for the first Temple to be cut and his son Solomon was the one who put it together (1 Chronicles 22:2). Pictures and models of it today based on Scripture, archaeology and history show a huge staircase at the front which was there to symbolise going up to meet with God (1 Kings 6:8). I always feel the stairway in the Temple leading to the place of praise, prayer, intercession and the holy of holies symbolises Jacob's ladder which leads to the presence of God. Whenever we ascend the steps to worship God we join with the angels in heaven, usually untroubled by snakes. Satan and his troops cannot bear to stay in a place where heartfelt worship of God is being expressed.

Jesus is the fulfilment of God's promise to David

After David's son Solomon died the people of God broke the first two commandments so regularly that the history of Israel from then on reads just like a loser playing the game of Snakes and Ladders. Instead of having no other gods and not creating any graven images they worshipped various Canaanite deities and bowed down to idols. The occasional ups during the reigns of people like David, Solomon and Josiah are more than overcome by the severe downs of kings like Rehoboam, Omri and Ahab.

The New Testament, however, begins with new hope: 'A record of the genealogy of Jesus Christ the son of David, the son of Abraham' (Matthew 1:1). For hundreds of years God has protected the family of Abraham and the dynasty of David so that two covenant promises made many years apart can be fulfilled in one man. Jesus, the son of Abraham and the son of David, has now arrived with healing for all humankind. In Luke the Angel Gabriel sets up the story of Jesus with this prophecy to Mary: 'The Lord God will give him the throne of his father David, and he will reign over the house of Jacob for ever; his kingdom will never end' (Luke 1:31-33).

Zechariah picked up the same theme in his song of praise to God: 'He has raised up a horn of salvation for us in the house of his servant David' (Luke 1:68-69).

The fulfilment of the prophecies about the Davidic kingship began to unfold as Jesus was born in Bethlehem, the town of David (Luke 2:11). It is an event which was seen to have universal significance as some Gentiles arrived asking: 'Where is the one who has been born King of the Jews? We saw his star in the east and have come to worship him' (Matthew 2:2). True worshippers of the king now come from all nations.

The timing of Jesus' kingly claim is very important. Early in the ministry of Jesus, John wrote: 'Jesus, knowing that they intended to come and make him king by force, withdrew again to a mountain by himself' (John 6:15). The people wanted a political king to free them from Caesar but Jesus is the spiritual king who frees us from Satan. Consequently Jesus waited until Palm Sunday before revealing his kingly identity by riding into Jerusalem on a donkey. This brought to fruition the prophecy of Zechariah 9:9 as quoted by Matthew. 'Say to the Daughter of Zion, "See, your king comes to you, gentle and riding on a donkey"' (Matthew 21:5).

The people obviously understood this implication. 'The crowds that went ahead of him and those that followed shouted, 'Hosanna to the Son of David!"' (Matthew 21:9). Afterwards Jesus described himself as the 'King' who would execute judgement at the end of time (Matthew 25:31,34,40) and at his trial admitted to being 'the King of the Jews' (Matthew 27:11; Luke 23:3), a title which was put on his cross (Matthew 27:37). In John's Gospel Jesus qualified the title by saying to Pilate: 'My kingdom is not of this world' (John 18:36) which Peter clarified further when he described the ascension of Jesus as the coronation of the King in heaven; a much greater king than David (Acts 2:32-36).

In David's day it was possible for the people to worship God with 'all their might' – mind, will, emotions and body (2 Samuel 6). Now, through the work and words of Jesus and the pouring out of his Spirit on all believers, we can also worship God in spirit and in truth (John 4:23-24). The truth of Scripture helps us to draw near to God with confidence knowing in our minds that because of Jesus we are God's children. The presence of his Holy Spirit in our lives helps us to worship God in spirit as we experience the full assurance of sins forgiven (Hebrews 10:19,22). Believing and receiving God's word and Spirit can take us up the temple stairway, through the torn curtain, into the throne room of grace, where in God's presence the desire within all of our spirits to be true worshippers can now be fully satisfied.

Many are cold but few are frozen

In 1985 I attended my first John Wimber Conference in Sheffield. There I experienced worship, word and ministry in the power of the Holy Spirit in a way I had never experienced before. God blew my socks off. I came back enthusiastically and simply had to take Roger with me the following year when part two was scheduled to take place in Harrogate. He graciously agreed to come.

 Roger is a very controlled human being not given to excesses of emotion and enthusiasm except when conducting a choir. The only time he has ever gone over on the floor in the power of the Holy Spirit was in Australia when he thought he was far enough away from home not to be noticed.

Roger enjoyed the worship at Harrogate. He kept telling me what key he thought they were in and how they modulated from one to another keeping the continuity flowing, but he was definitely with it and participating. He enjoyed the jokes, the practical teaching and the exposition of God's word which he found to be generally sound and helpful. Our beloved composer felt the ministry was very powerful, very loving and very effective for everyone else who was there.

'Maybe,' he thought, 'if Peter and I don't sit together we would be less inhibited and God's blessings would have more runway on which to land.' Our separation experiment proved to be very interesting.

John invited us all to stand as he asked God to send his Holy Spirit on us. As God moved most powerfully the normally placid unruffled personality of Roger suddenly broke out into a fearful, cold sweat. He looked and felt like an underdressed Brit in an Ottawa winter becoming paralysed and frozen to the spot. Wimber hadn't covered this kind of manifestation in his teaching and those around Roger couldn't remember any Scripture verses about icebergs in the Holy Land. A friend came to get me so I could see this strange sight which had come to pass.

Meanwhile Roger began registering pictures of people he knew as they flashed across his mind like photographs in an album. Each one was a person who struggled with worship, particularly the more 'modern' approach of King David which involved will, emotions and body as well as 'mind' and spirit. We did what any sensible person would do in such a situation and went to find an American; one of those liberated, full-flowing, gregarious, no-holds-barred type of personalities. We managed to get a ministry team member from California who quickly discerned what God was doing.

'This is God giving you a dramatic word of knowledge,' he said, 'relating to how some people feel about true worship. It will help you in your music ministry to sit where others are sitting.'

We wondered about leaving Roger in the freezer while the rest of us escaped for a meal but he thawed out in time to come with us. The experience has proved to be very helpful to him ever since. Roger is often invited to minister to groups who come from traditional and sometimes purely musical backgrounds. He can mix augmented ninths and diminished sevenths with the best of them, but irrespective of musical style and theological tradition, Roger believes in trying to help people become 'true worshippers' in body, mind, will, emotions and spirit. Frequently he likes inviting God to send his Holy Spirit to help them do this, and frequently he needs great sensitivity in helping people who find it difficult to receive. This I believe is Roger's anointed ministry, confirmed and empowered by God in Harrogate.

 The Temple stairway was built for people to go up into the presence of God. There they could be cleansed from sin, pray and worship. The alternative society offered to the world by the Christian Church will always seek to be a place of confession, prayer and true worship.

GROUP STUDY *True worshippers*

 A theological question: 'The Lord came and stood there, calling as at other times, "Samuel! Samuel!"' (1 Samuel 3:10). Who is the Lord?
Read John 4:16-26.

1. How did Jesus know the woman was a sinner? (John 4:17-19).
2. Why did Jesus talk to such a notorious sinner? What should our attitude be in dealing with sinners? (John 8:7-11).
3. Should we welcome people who are not married but living together, to worship with us in church?

4. How important was the place of worship to Jesus? (John 4:21-24).

5. How may we worship in truth? (John 4:23-24).

6. How may we worship in spirit? (John 4:23-24).

7. How may we become true worshippers? (John 4:23-24).

8 A SNAKE THAT BITES
The minor prophets

All seemed well at the beginning of the marriage. Here were two young people with everything to live for anticipating a lifetime of being together. Their closest friends, however, always suspected that her commitment was much more nominal than his. She was the one far more in tune with the world, and at times parties, alcohol, silver and gold came nearer to the centre of her heart than her husband or God.

Even before their first child came along he began to harbour doubts about her loyalty and faithfulness to him. When a son was born it ought to have been a time of great rejoicing and thanksgiving but he found himself having to deal with feelings of anger and revenge at the naming ceremony. Being a godly man he pushed it down, coped remarkably well and struggled to make his own misgivings and fears a matter of privacy.

When the second child, a girl, was born, his love for his wife was definitely growing cold. He knew all about his lifetime promise to love and cherish her in the good times and the bad, no matter what happened, and as a believer in God, love and truth, he kept his word. He stood loyally by his wife in public and at home but the feeling inside was one of duty rather than love, and his heart was full of pain.

By the time the third child came along, a boy, he was pretty sure this was not his child. Whispers, rumours, circumstances and the tell-tale signs are always there, if ever one wants to know the truth and face up to it. In the end she left him and went to live with the other man.

The grass is not always greener on the other side and sometimes, after a while, reconciliation and a returning to old pastures becomes possible. What price getting her back? Surely not a wise or sensible move after the way she'd treated him? What price love, forgiveness and mercy for the true believer who only loves because God first loved him or her? The world would have none of it. Even if she was willing to come back she wasn't worth it. Look at the shame and disgrace she'd already caused him and would undoubtedly do again given half a chance. At such moments it was tempting for him to ask what his friends would think, especially the religious ones, but he knew in his heart of hearts they would probably all respond, 'Enough is enough.'

In his quiet times, his precious moments alone with God, the voice of the world began to fade after he'd worshipped and meditated on God's word. He sensed the voice of God telling him not to give up and to be prepared to take her back. Love is never cheap, but discerning the right moment he eventually paid the price and took her home to live with him again.

As a prophet, Hosea knew the word of God, but in the sadness of his own married life he also sensed the compassion of God and felt some of his pain towards Israel whom God had loved like a faithful husband. Time and time again Israel was unfaithful to God and broke her marriage covenant with him, but time and time again, when she was willing to return, God paid the price of love and received her back. Now, however, her chasing after other lovers had gone too far and judgement needed to be announced.

Judgement

 Hosea named his first child Jezreel after the town where much blood had been spilt. 'Then the Lord said to Hosea, "Call him Jezreel, because I will soon punish the house of Jehu for the massacre at Jezreel, and I will put an end to the kingdom of Israel. In that day I will break Israel's bow in the Valley of Jezreel"' (Hosea 1:4-5).

The Lord told Hosea to call his second child 'Lo-Ruhamah' (not pitied), 'for I will no longer show love to the house of Israel' (Hosea 1:6).

The third child was given the name, 'Lo-Ammi' (not my people). 'Then the Lord said, "Call him Lo-Ammi, for you are not my people, and I am not your God"' (Hosea 1:9).

Through the names of the prophet's children God declared that the Northern Kingdom of Israel was coming to an end because of her sin.

Hosea, like Amos, Elijah and Elisha, prophesied in the Northern Kingdom of Israel. After Solomon died, Jeroboam, one of Solomon's officials, led a revolt against Rehoboam the son of Solomon, and all Israel except the tribes of Judah and Benjamin followed him. They rebelled 'against the house of David' and made Jeroboam their king (1 Kings 12:19). He in turn set up two religious shrines; one at Bethel where Jacob had seen the ladder in a dream, and one in Dan, further north. Each one had a golden calf, and Jeroboam 'appointed priests from all sorts of people, even though they were not Levites'.

Consequently their religion began to resemble the local Canaanite religions which eventually included prostitution and child sacrifice (1 Kings 12:31).

The kings in the Northern Kingdom were not necessarily descendants of David. After Jeroboam died Baasha killed all his descendants and grabbed the throne; Zimri took it from Baasha's son and Omri took it from Zimri. Omri built his capital city at Samaria where his son Ahab reigned for twenty-two years, but Ahab was the worst of the lot, married Jezebel from Sidonia, and built a temple for Baal in Samaria.

Elijah and Elisha were used by God to oppose Ahab, to challenge people to confess and repent of their sins, to believe in Yahweh, and to anoint Jehu as the Davidic king who would destroy all Ahab's descendants. Jehu was the son of the good king Jehoshophat from Jerusalem, a descendant of David, and his family reigned in Samaria for four generations. Unfortunately none of them put right the sins of Jeroboam I, and Jehu's grandson, Jeroboam II, 'did evil in the eyes of the Lord' (2 Kings 14:24). It was during his forty-one-year reign in Samaria that Hosea and Amos brought God's messages to the people. Just like Hosea, Amos said God was going to put an end to the Northern Kingdom because of the people's sins since the time of Jeroboam I.

Amos put it like this. 'It will be as though a man entered . . . his house and rested his hand on the wall only to have a snake bite him' (Amos 5:19). The snake was to be the cruel and powerful Assyrians whom God would not prevent from invading the Northern Kingdom and taking them into exile. Consequently, because the people were unfaithful to God again and again, over many generations the snake was going to bite as in the days of Noah, Sodom and Gomorrah and Pharaoh, king of Egypt. It all reads like a judge's irreversible sentence but maybe somewhere, some way, there was still hope for Israel. What price getting her back?

In Charles Dickens' novel, *A Christmas Carol*, Ebenezer

Scrooge asked the prophetic spirit, 'Are these the shadows of the things that *will* be, or are they shadows of the things that *may* be only?' It is a question also worth asking of God's prophecy to Hosea. The answer begins with the character of God.

Love

The love of God is mentioned in many books of the Old Testament but Hosea is one of the first to major on this theme. Maybe it was because in the sadness of his own life he felt the true compassion of God more than others. In the following famous passage the picture changes from husband and wife to father and son but the same love of God is beautifully expressed.

> When Israel was a child, I loved him, and out of Egypt I called my son. But the more I called Israel, the further they went from me. They sacrificed to the Baals and they burned incense to images. It was I who taught Ephraim to walk, taking them by the arms; but they did not realise it was I who healed them. I led them with cords of human kindness, with ties of love; I lifted the yoke from their neck and bent down to feed them.
>
> (Hosea 11:1-4)

This compassionate nature of God gave a flicker of hope to the people of the Northern Kingdom (Ephraim), despite the apparently unconditional condemnation of them (Hosea 1). Understanding the true nature of God's prophecy also added to the possibility of a reprieve.

Repentance

The prophets did not speak merely to predict the future but to encourage sinful people to turn from their evil ways and to turn once more to the Law of

God. 'Forth-telling' rather than 'foretelling' is the way it is normally put. The equivalent today would be seen as preaching God's truths from the Bible. The Old Testament prophets spoke God's word to try and bring the people back to their own covenant promises and responsibilities, believing that if they returned to God his love would cause him to grant them mercy.

After Hosea's children were given symbolical names which spelt doom and disaster for Israel (Hosea 1) his wife left him. This represented the separation between God, the faithful husband, and Israel, the unfaithful wife. But in chapter three Hosea was told, 'Go, show your love to your wife again' (Hosea 3:1), which he understood to mean buying her back. By analogy this action revealed God's willingness to welcome Israel's return to him, consequently, in the last chapter of Hosea the prophet still urged his people to repent:

> Return, O Israel, to the Lord your God. Your sins have been your downfall! Take words with you and return to the Lord. Say to him: 'Forgive all our sins and receive us graciously, that we may offer the fruit of our lips. Assyria cannot save us; we will not mount war-horses. We will never again say "Our gods" to what our own hands have made, for in you the fatherless find compassion.'
>
> (Hosea 14:1-3)

With God hope always springs eternal. Although God said the Northern Kingdom would be destroyed, Hosea kept preaching repentance even in his final chapter. This is consistent with God's message found in some of the other minor prophets.

Jonah, proclaimed this word from the Lord. 'Forty more days and Nineveh will be overturned' (Jonah 3:4). It proved to be one of the most successful prophecies of all time even though it didn't come true. The king and people of the evil and violent capital city of Assyria believed God, repented in sackcloth and dust, and Nineveh survived. Jonah was furious that God failed to keep his word, but God said compassion was more important. It is not always possible to know the future from God's prophecies, but it *is* always possible to know his character and heart. He loves his people and repeatedly meets confession and repentance with forgiveness. The minor prophets consistently denounce sin on God's behalf but point to his love and mercy for those who turn from it.

Sadly, the children of Israel from the Northern Kingdom did not repent and 'in the ninth year of Hoshea, the king of Assyria captured Samaria and deported the Israelites to Assyria . . . All this took place because the Israelites had sinned against the Lord' (2 Kings 17:6-7). This was just over forty years after Jeroboam II died and there is no evidence they ever returned.

Jesus and prophecy

St Matthew sees the birth of Jesus in Bethlehem as the fulfilment of a prophecy given by another minor prophet, Micah. 'But you, Bethlehem, in the land of Judah, are by no means least among the rulers of Judah; for out of you will come a ruler who will be the shepherd of my people Israel' (Matthew 2:6). The new hope for all the world is born in Bethlehem as the prophets foretold.

Jesus fulfils many words from the Old Testament prophets, both minor and major, some of which I have included in Appendix 4.

As a prophet himself Jesus proclaims the word of God fearlessly, just like the minor prophets, and the first part of his message is unchanging.

Hosea said repent (Hosea 11:5;14:1-2); Joel said repent (Joel 2:12); Amos said repent (Amos 5:14-15); Jonah caused people to repent (Jonah 3:16); Zechariah said repent (Zechariah 1:3); and John the Baptist told the people in Jesus' day to repent (Matthew 3:2). Jesus begins his ministry by proclaiming the need to repent (Mark 1:15); after his resurrection he commissions the disciples to preach 'repentance and forgiveness of sins' to all nations (Luke 24:45-47); and on the day when Jesus poured out the Holy Spirit on his disciples, Peter stood up and told everyone to repent (Acts 2:38). The character of God never changes and the Christian Church has the responsibility to proclaim the same message from God's word, the Bible, to all people.

The second part of Jesus' message, however, moves into a new dimension. The prophets told people to repent in order to avoid exile, and to find political peace, prosperity and victory over the other nations. But Jesus said, 'Repent and believe the good news' so that we may enter the kingdom of God and receive eternal life (Mark 1:15; John 3:5,16). Peter, on the day of Pentecost, uses Joel, another minor prophet, to announce that the Jesus' community, made up of those who repent, enter the kingdom of God and receive new life in the power of the Holy Spirit, will be full of prophets:

> In the last days, God says, I will pour out my Spirit on all people. Your sons and daughters will prophesy, your young men will see visions, your old men will dream dreams. Even on my servants, both men and women, I will pour out my Spirit in those days, and they will prophesy.
>
> (Acts 2:17-18)

Men and women, young and old will be prophetically gifted and equipped when they are filled with the Spirit of Jesus.

A prophetic people

The Church as an alternative Jesus society will always be based on the word of God. Primarily the Bible as the unchanging word of God tells us about the character of God, the way we can have a relationship with him, be saved and filled with his Holy Spirit. This never changes. What does change, however, is the day-to-day guidance for which God has given us the Holy Spirit. A community which is based on the truth of the Bible will also expect to hear God speaking and 'be eager to prophesy' so that they may know God's guidance for today (1 Corinthians 14:39). When Amos and Hosea said exile was coming, this was guidance by God's Spirit for their day. Today, we who believe in Jesus are filled with the same Holy Spirit, all have access to the 'mind of Christ' and can be guided by him (1 Corinthians 2:11-16).

Guidance

 When Roger Jones left the Birmingham School of Music he became a music teacher in a comprehensive school at Aston. As a Christian he tried to use his music to bring the gospel of Jesus Christ to the pupils, but it was not easy. The obvious way was to perform Christian songs at Christmas concerts or to stage musicals with Christian words. There were some biblical stories set to music such as Noah, Joseph, Jonah and Daniel but the lyrics were not particularly Christian.

At lunch-time one day the headmaster heard Roger doodling on the piano, improvising around a minor third, and suggested he wrote it as a song. Thus encouraged, 'Jesus rode a donkey into town' came into being followed by an entire Easter musical now called *Jerusalem Joy*. If there were no suitable Christian musicals to use at school why not write your own? So Roger did. At one stage a quarter of the school was in the choir.

The musical was a hit at school, at the local church, and eventually with national publishers. Churches which had annual Sunday school concerts were particularly keen on it, but then so were many others as new, popular music for Easter is welcome in many churches.

Interest grew quickly as Roger discovered a gifting, an anointing and a market. The story of Pentecost, *Saints Alive*, was the first specifically adult work aimed more at churches than schools and this opened up another opportunity in the community for putting on Roger's works. The aim behind them all was to present the good news of God's word in an entertaining way, which was enjoyable and easy to receive. Meanwhile Roger was promoted at work and became the head of lower school.

The East Birmingham Renewal Group (EBRG) was formed after Roger conducted a performance of *Come Together*, written by Jimmy and Carol Owens, to try and promote renewal, often through Christian music, in East Birmingham. After a while it developed into a support group for Roger as the demand for his own musicals increased and Carol and I were delighted to become members of this group.

Pressures of work, increased demands from the Christian community for Roger, and a recognition that God had given him distinctive skills often led to discussion about him going full-time. It never amounted to much and at times came across like the idea of 'one day writing my memoirs' but neither would it lie down and die.

The moment when it became more serious from my point of view was the day when Roger was going to conduct a big performance in the town hall of one of his works. He was not well and had a bad throat, so he took the day off from school in order to be fit enough for the musical.

''Ello! 'Ello!' I thought to myself. 'Is this a good witness? Is this the right thing for a Christian to be doing? If Roger's heart is more in doing musicals than teaching at school should he really be in teaching?'

I chatted to friends and I raised my concerns. I remember talking to an experienced clergyman from the cathedral who advised caution. He'd seen many Christians who felt they had a 'ministry' or a 'calling' leave a good job, put their family at risk, depend for a while on Christians to bale them out and then fall flat on their faces. It was good to talk and at EBRG I talked about it at length.

Christmas came and I was ill – bad head, bad cold, bad throat – probably caught it from Roger. I went to bed the day before one of our Christmas services, drugged up to the eyeballs, with no faith in God for healing but I still cried out to him for help.

'Never mind about your aches and pains,' he seemed to say. 'It is time for Roger to go full time.'

'Oh yea!' I thought. 'What about all the friends of the canon from the cathedral? They all thought God said that too.' Silence reigned.

'OK,' I said, 'but how do I know it's you? This is serious stuff.'

'In a while,' he seemed to say, 'you'll go to sleep. You will have a good night's sleep. You'll be woken by sunlight streaming through the curtains. You'll be well enough to do all the Christmas services and I will pave the way practically for Roger once you've started the ball rolling.'

I felt dreadful. It was pouring with rain and the forecast was worse. If I woke healed on a glorious sunny day with a cheque for £50,000 on the mat I'd take it as guidance. I reacted quite negatively at the time to the whole thing but eventually went to sleep.

I slept all through the night, woke up feeling a little better and with a bright light shining in my face. Our curtains didn't close too well and through a gap a couple of centimetres wide the sun was beaming through. I rose and went to the window. It was cloudy everywhere but for just ten minutes there was a tiny break in the clouds which the sun pierced, striking through a tiny chink in our curtains and bringing illumination to my countenance. After that it rained quite hard all day. Mentioning the early morning sun to my friends later made them think my mind was being affected by my cold. I actually didn't feel too bad, was fine for all the Christmas services but there was no money on the carpet.

I shared it all with Roger and together we agreed to talk it over with the group. Roger himself was studying Nehemiah at the time. It's a wonderful story from the Bible of how Nehemiah, cupbearer to the king of Persia, asked for leave of absence to go to Jerusalem where the city was still in ruins. He asked for a letter to get him safe conduct and timber for rebuilding the city wall and residences. What a nerve! 'And because the gracious hand of my God was upon me, the king granted my requests' (Nehemiah 2:8). The Bible is invaluable in teaching us how God does things. We didn't think we needed letters from a king or lorries full of logs at the time but the principles of Scripture seemed good to us. If God calls you, God will provide. It is the character of God.

The group agreed to test the waters. By now Roger had considerable mailing lists of people who regularly attended his events so we wrote to all of them and asked for their opinions. We received many different replies but our response to the responses was perhaps our strongest leading. We read through all the ideas, arguments and counter arguments. We came together and prayed without seeing an angel, writing on the wall or hearing a voice thundering from heaven but together we were of one mind. Roger was disappointed. He wanted to be sure. He wanted a sign.

'Right,' I said. 'We'll give you one. We'll go round the room, ask everyone what they think and take a vote.' It was unanimous. We all agreed to put Roger's head on the chopping block. 'There you are,' I said. 'The body of Christ, full of the Spirit of God, having prayed to God and waited upon him are of one mind.' I think Roger preferred Nehemiah to us but he eventually accepted the consensus. We then did two things.

1. I wrote to everyone on the mailing list on behalf of EBRG to see if there would be any prayer or financial sup-

port. This had two disastrous consequences. Someone gave a copy of the letter to Roger's dad who was furious, and a second relative thought my request of £10,000 a year for a man with four children, a mortgage and need of a car to travel around was exorbitant for a Christian.

Harold Jones had struggled to survive in the twenties and thirties. A job was a job even if you hated it and it was the responsibility of every father to provide for his family without begging. Roger's dad used to play the piano for our over-sixties' social club but, after seeing the letter, he never came again. Mary Jones, however, couldn't see what all the fuss was about. She thought it was right and Roger should give it a go.

2. Roger decided to write to the king and ask for two years' leave of absence. This may have been all right for Persia, but the chief education officer in Birmingham was a different matter. Such a request was unheard of at the time, even though it was well supported by Roger's headmaster.

Some people responded positively to my letter and some money and covenants were promised but it was the king who was amazing. Two years' leave of absence was granted so that if it didn't work out Roger could have his job back as head of lower school. This response was like the final rung of a springboard ladder which encouraged Roger to have a prayerful go.

Writing musicals, doing weekends for churches plus the generosity of individuals meant that after one year Roger was doing as well financially as when he'd been teaching. He was now doing a very specialised work which God seemed to have anointed in many ways. In the second year the work and ministry continued to go well and we all relaxed until Roger received a call from his headmaster. 'I need to know if you're coming back,' he began. 'If I have to find a new head of lower school I must start making plans now.'

Even though everything was going nicely this was the costly moment when the boats needed burning. If you pray, take advice from the body of Christ, and God seems to answer with signs following; it is very difficult for people of faith to go back, so we went forward.

At the beginning only Roger was employed but now, after just over fifteen years, three people are earning a reasonable salary from the work. At times the cupboard has been pretty bare but EBRG kept this from Roger so as not to stifle his creativity. We never wanted him to write or do things simply for money, but only for God. I think it is fair to say Roger has reached many people with the gospel through song who might not otherwise have heard it and a number of people have been better equipped through his ministry in worshipping God.

It is never easy to discover God's guidance clearly and unmistakably and we still need many more Christian teachers in our schools, but weighing up Roger's abilities and anointing, the signs along the way, the agreement of Scripture, the affirmation of the Spirit-filled body of Christ and God's generous provision, I believe God helped Roger and Mary to get this one right. I think Harold was beginning to think so too before he died.

The Christian Church is called upon to declare the eternal truths of the Bible to all people and our lives and church activities should be governed by God's inspired word just as  the minor prophets were. The Bible, however, does not give us day-to-day guidance and for this we need to learn together to discern the inner voice of God's Spirit as Amos and Hosea did. The alternative society of Christ's body here on earth was always meant to be a prophetic people.

GROUP STUDY *Prophecy*

A powerful question: Who is the strongest person in the Old Testament?
Read John 13:18-38.

1. Why did Jesus quote Psalm 41:9? (John 13:18).
2. Why did Jesus prophesy about Judas? (John 13:19. See also Appendix 1).
3. During the Passover meal it is traditional for the president to dip the sop and give it to the person he loves the most. Why do you think Jesus gave it to Judas? (John 13:26).
4. Why does John write, 'And it was night'? (John 13:30. See John 12:35-36). Could Judas have been forgiven?
5. How many commandments are there in the Bible? Which one is the hardest? (John 13:34).
6. Why does Jesus prophesy about his departure? (John 13:33). Why did Thomas not understand? (John 14:5).
7. Why did Jesus predict Peter's denial? (John 13:38). Can we prophesy today? How could it help the Church?

9 SNAKES WITH VENOM
The suffering servant

How deserted lies the city once so full of people! How like a widow is she! Bitterly she weeps at night. Streams of tears overflow unceasingly from her eyes without relief.

Mount Zion lies desolate with jackals prowling over it. Her gates have sunk into the earth; her bars broken and destroyed. The strongholds, ramparts and walls have wasted away and her buildings swallowed up. Palaces have been brought down to the ground and the Temple laid waste like a garden. The altar is rejected, her sanctuary abandoned and the enemy has laid hands on all her treasures.

The sword bereaves. Young and old lie together in the dust of the streets. Young men and maidens have fallen by the sword; priests and prophets killed in the sanctuary of the

Lord. Women have been ravished in Zion, and virgins in the towns of Judah. Princes have been hung up by their hands, their bodies blacker than soot and their skin shrivelled on their bones.

Those killed by the sword are better off than those who die of famine; racked with hunger, they waste away for lack of nourishment from the fields. All Zion's people groan as they search for bread; they barter their treasures for food to keep themselves alive. Priests and elders perish in the city as they look for sustenance while the lives of children and infants ebb away in their mothers' arms. With their own hands compassionate women have cooked and eaten their children.

After affliction and harsh labour, Judah has gone into exile. Her children, her young men and maidens, her king and her princes have been taken to Babylon. Her enemies look at Jerusalem and laugh at her destruction. Her teeth have been broken with gravel and she has been trampled in the dust. Mocked in song she has become the laughing-stock of the nations.

Look and see if there is any suffering like her suffering. Is it nothing to you, all you who pass by?

Has God utterly rejected Jerusalem? Is he angry with her beyond measure?

(Adapted from the book of Lamentations in the Old Testament.)

Nebuchadnezzar, King of Babylon, laid siege to the city of Jerusalem and King Jehoiachin surrendered. The king, the soldiers and the craftsmen were all taken into exile together with the gold from the Temple and the royal palace.

Zedekiah was made king in Jerusalem and allowed to reign over all that was left but after nine years he rebelled against Nebuchadnezzar who then marched to the scene with his army. Jerusalem, built on a hill, was very cleverly designed with only one narrow entrance which could be held by a few against many. 'The kings of the earth did not believe, nor did any of the world's people, that enemies and foes could enter the gates of Jerusalem' (Lamentations 4:12). The Babylonians, therefore, camped outside the city for two years until the famine inside became severe and nothing was left.

At this point Zedekiah and his followers tried to escape but all were captured in the process. The Temple, the palace and the houses in Jerusalem were burnt down and everyone but the poorest people were taken to Babylon with any remaining articles of value. There they killed all the sons of Zedekiah in front of him before putting out his own eyes.

Lamentations is the lament of the poor people left behind. The exile affected every Jew from Jerusalem, good or bad. Daniel, Shadrach, Meshach, Abednego, Jeremiah, Ezekiel and maybe an Isaiah or two suffered with all other Judaeans. Sometimes people who love God and seek to serve him suffer just like everyone else.

Fears in the silence

On a non-cup-final day in July 1972, Roger Jones and Mary were married. They became the proud parents of four sons and a daughter and enjoyed worshipping God together. In 1991 Mary had a mole removed surgically from her back. In 1992 she spotted a growth under her left armpit which the doctor said was nothing to worry about, but by April 1994 Mary felt continually weary and still had the lump so she was referred to a specialist. In the June a biopsy took place which revealed some abnormal cells, and the words 'possible cancer' were gently brought into the conversation. The medical advice was to have the growth removed at which point many Christian friends began praying.

'Fears in the silence' were how Roger and Mary described it. Waiting, praying, hoping, getting on with life, but with the fears for ever there in their minds waiting to leap upon them in unguarded moments. At times the nights were very long and drawn-out and when another postman's pile of mail landed on the doormat without the medical invitation the days were long as well. It felt like living in Jerusalem with the Babylonians camped outside.

The appointment for the operation eventually came through with a November date when Roger was due to be doing another tour of Canada. This time there was no need for discussion among close friends and supporters as Roger cancelled the tour immediately. Sometimes God tests us and asks us to be willing to make sacrifices and sometimes we have to make them. Roger made himself available to give Mary his undivided attention.

The lump was removed successfully but it was followed by more waiting and wondering until the specialist was ready to see them. When he did manage to fit them into his busy schedule, words like 'malignant' and, 'secondary melanoma' were used as the surgeon drew them a spectrum diagram. 'Those at this end,' he said, 'cannot be helped at all because the cancer has gone too far. Those at the other end,' he continued, 'can be cured completely. You,' he suggested, looking at Mary, 'are somewhere in between.' She would be referred to a skin specialist who would give her a CT scan in an effort to find the source of the primary growth.

Mary is a nurse and knew the prognosis was not that hopeful. Cancer in the lymph gland is very virulent and when it spreads to all of the other glands is known as Hodgkin's disease. Roger gave me a ring and he and Mary came to stay with us in Dorset for a few days.

I've read a lot of Christian books on healing and written one or two myself. I'm not very good at it but I know a bit about it. I thought they'd want the laying-on-of-hands, maybe some anointing with oil, a touch of emotional healing and possibly a spot of deliverance here and there. That's what Christians do when they're ill don't they? How wrong can you be? There's a time and a season for throwing everything into prayer for healing and this wasn't it.

When the news breaks the first stage for many is coming to

terms with reality. I am mortal. One day I will die. Now I may die sooner rather than later. I need to enter my own Gethsemane where Jesus prayed on the eve of Good Friday, to make my own peace with the prospect of death. It's the place of truth. Sometimes to talk immediately about healing whether through surgery, prayer or both is to seek an escape from the pain. The mature Christian way which I've been privileged to observe in many of God's suffering servants is to face the pain with Christ, seeking to come through it rather than to run away from it. This may lead to healing or it may not, but either way it leads to Christ.

Roger and Mary spent time with each other and they never asked us for ministry. Walking hand in hand on the deserted beach and taking in the beauty of coastal Dorset was the order of the day. It appeared to an onlooker as though thankfulness for the life God had given them so far, together, was most important in coming to terms with the present. The future, it seemed, was for tomorrow.

They went home refreshed and I suspect closer to one another and to God while my so-called knowledge, books and theories were left for another day. On this occasion prayer was all-sufficient as there was good news waiting for them.

The CT scan showed no signs of cancer anywhere else so Mary was booked in to have the troublesome lymph gland removed. Apparently our tonsils are also lymph glands and we can manage without one or two of them quite easily. Much prayer continued and the operation took place just before Christmas. In due course Mary's strength returned and subsequent scans showed no further signs of cancer. The two-monthly check-ups became four-monthly and now four years on have become six-monthly. As I write Mary feels well and full of gratitude to God.

On the day I took some notes from Roger and Mary for this chapter, they attended the funeral of a life-long Christian friend who was five years younger than Mary. Merilyn died of cancer. Christians are not always excused the pains and traumas of life but they do have Christ with them to help them face suffering and go through it.

In exile

The big theological questions now needed to be asked in Babylon itself.

a) Is God dead?

Has Marduk, the god of the Babylonians, defeated Yahweh the God of the Jews and if not, is Yahweh still their God or has he utterly rejected them? Shadrach, Meshach, Abednego and Daniel went into exile as young men with the first group. They still obeyed God's laws and refused to bow down to idols so Shadrach, Meshach and Abednego were thrown in the fiery furnace and Daniel into the lions' den. When God miraculously delivered all four of them a new theology began to dawn. Even though the Temple which housed God's footstool, and the city where the Temple was situated, were both destroyed, Yahweh was still alive and well (Lamentations 2:1). Even though it took a fiery furnace and a lions' den to discover it, 'I AM' was still the God of the Jews who obeyed him and followed him, even in exile.

When the believing Jews looked at the gods of Babylon they laughed. They were only made of wood, metal and stone. They answered their tormentors very simply.

> Why do the nations say, 'Where is their God?' Our God is in heaven; he does whatever pleases him. But their idols are silver and gold, made by the hands of men. They have mouths, but cannot speak, eyes, but they cannot see; they have ears, but cannot hear, noses, but they cannot smell. They have hands, but cannot feel, feet, but they cannot walk; nor can they utter a sound with their throats.
>
> (Psalm 115:2-7)

The gods of Babylon were no gods at all.

b) If God is not dead – why did he not save us?

The history of the Southern Kingdom was researched and recorded as a pretty evenly contested game of Snakes and Ladders between good and evil. It started with Rehoboam, son of Solomon, who was a snake. 'My father scourged you with whips,' he said. 'I will scourge you with scorpions' (1 Kings 12:14). This idea was not well received and the Kingdom became divided, but after that the Southern Kingdom of Judah, based at Jerusalem, had a number of very good ladders.

Perhaps the most amazing ladder was the family tree of the kings. David's line was continued right through to Jehoiachin, who surrendered to Babylon, with every king succeeded by his son. It came very close to termination when Joash's grandma tried to kill all David's descendants but Joash was smuggled out of the death chamber and eventually crowned king at the age of seven (2 Kings 11:1-21).

There were eight kings who 'did what was right in the eyes of the Lord' and between them they reigned for 263 years. Jerusalem was saved by God from the Assyrians, who destroyed the Northern Kingdom, through prayer and prophecy in the reign of Hezekiah and there were some particularly blessed times in the days of Jehoshaphat, Joash and Josiah.

Unfortunately in between these significant ladders there were some very venomous snakes. Jehoram married the daughter of evil King Ahab from Samaria and came under his influence. Ahaz sacrificed his own son, others set up idols and worshipped them and then there was Manasseh who reigned for fifty-five years. Although he may have found personal forgiveness at the end of his life, the evil which he did during the longest reign of Israel's history affected the people and the nation very deeply.

King Josiah 'turned to the Lord' and 'got rid of the mediums and spiritists, the household gods, the idols and all the other detestable things seen in Judah and Jerusalem' (2 Kings 23:24-25). The prophet Jeremiah welcomed the reforms at first, and hoped they would lead to true repentance for the whole nation, but they never did. A good king can change the outward ceremonies but not the hearts of his people. The last four kings of Judah all did evil in God's sight and the game was lost.

The conclusion of the historical research was this:

> The Lord, the God of their fathers, sent word to them through his messengers again and again, because he had pity on his people and on his dwelling-place. But they mocked God's messengers, despised his words and scoffed at his prophets until the wrath of the Lord was aroused against his people and there was no remedy (2 Chronicles 36:15-16).
>
> It was because of the Lord's anger that all this happened to Jerusalem and Judah, and in the end he thrust them from his presence (2 Kings 24:20).

According to Jeremiah they broke the Old Covenant and were punished by God for their wickedness.

c) Is there any hope?

The three major prophets, Jeremiah, Ezekiel and Isaiah, all prophesied a return from exile, a new hope, a new covenant and a new Messiah. In his time Jeremiah was never accepted as a major prophet from God but in exile Daniel found his book (Daniel 9:2). In it he described the impending doom and destruction of Jerusalem like the bites of venomous snakes.

' "I will send venomous snakes among you, vipers that cannot be charmed, and they will bite you," declares the Lord'

(Jeremiah 8:17). It reads very much like the snakes who bit the Hebrews in the desert just after Aaron died and the snake which bit the Northern Kingdom in  Samaria, but Jeremiah also said the Jews would return from Babylon after seventy years. This great hope inspired Daniel to confess and repent for the sins of his people and pray to God for deliverance (Daniel 9:4-19).

Ezekiel saw the famous valley of dry bones which God explained represented the people of Israel in exile. As Ezekiel prophesied the bones came together, flesh appeared and breath entered them. 'I will bring you back to the land of Israel,' said God (Ezekiel 37:12).

Isaiah of the exile began to speak prophetically into the lessons that were being learnt. The Jews had suffered double for all her sins and he was able to identify these five purposes which had emerged from it.

1. No other gods
Once they had been told, 'You shall have no other gods' (Exodus 20:3), now they *knew* there were no other gods (Isaiah 45:18). Theoretically this had always been the case, particularly as seen in the account of creation, but practically many Judaeans had lived as though all gods had something to offer. It seems as if their experience of 'no other gods' was important in sealing this truth for many of them.

2. King of the universe
The next logical step from this experience was to declare that Yahweh was the one, true, universal God, king of the universe; king in Jerusalem; king in Babylon (Isaiah 45:5-7).

3. A light to the Gentiles
This brought the universal covenant made with Abraham back into focus. The chosen people were not meant to keep Yahweh and his blessings to themselves. If he is the God of all

peoples then he must be shared with all peoples. The Jews were meant to be a light to the Gentiles and this found expression in the servant songs of Isaiah (Isaiah 42:6; 49:6).

4. No more idolatry

When the children of Israel returned to Jerusalem idolatry became a thing of the past. The exile in Babylon, though tragic, brought about a purifying and a cleansing from idol worship (Isaiah 44:6-21).

5. Redemptive suffering

And this put a whole new perspective on blessings and cursings because good came out of suffering. The value of redemptive suffering began to go alongside, if not to replace, the simplistic prosperity gospel which had gone before. In the early days God taught his children, 'Follow me and you will prosper.' Now they had learnt more of God and his ways it became, 'Follow me and others will prosper.' In this fallen world there will be times when God's people may have to suffer in order for God's purposes to be achieved. It paved the way for the suffering servant.

Jesus is the suffering servant

In the book of Isaiah we find four 'servant songs'. It looks as if Isaiah in his first servant song wonders if Israel's suffering servanthood might bring salvation to the world (Isaiah 42:6). In the second, probably because he knows too many unbelievers, he moves on to see the servant-role being carried out by a believing remnant, an Israel within Israel, of God's chosen people (Isaiah 49:6). When he arrives at the third servant song he now believes the servant will have to be himself; the only one sufficiently anointed by God to accomplish the task (Isaiah 50:4-5). But by the time he comes to the fourth and most famous song he is describing someone who is taking away even Isaiah's sin (Isaiah 53:6). He seems to realise that neither Israel, nor a remnant of Israel, nor even himself is capable of fulfilling this task. Instead, with prophetic inspired vision, he sees another, a sinless individual, a suffering servant who will bear the iniquity of us all. So sure is he that this will come to pass that he uses the prophetic past, writing as if it had already happened.

> He was despised and rejected by men, a man of sorrows and familiar with suffering . . . Surely he took up our infirmities and carried our sorrows, yet we considered him stricken by God, smitten by him, and afflicted. But he was pierced for our transgressions, he was crushed for our iniquities; the punishment that brought us peace was upon him, and by his wounds we are healed. We all, like sheep, have gone astray, each of us has turned to his own way; and the Lord has laid on him the iniquity of us all.
>
> (Isaiah 53:3-6)

It is difficult to read the New Testament and fail to notice that this sinless, perfect, redemptive suffering has been accomplished by Jesus Christ. His flawless life, his ministry of healing, his death on the cross, his resurrection and ascension fit this prophetic song in virtually every detail. Philip certainly saw Jesus as the fulfilment of this passage (Acts 8:32-35).

The followers of Christ

Only the perfect Son of God could die for the sins of the world on the cross. His death at Calvary is unique just as he is unique and yet we who belong to Christ are also called, to some extent, to be suffering servants. This is what Jesus promised his followers:

Then Jesus said to his disciples, 'If anyone would come after me, he must deny himself and take up his cross and follow me.'

(Matthew 16:24)

'You will be handed over to be persecuted and put to death, and you will be hated by all nations because of me.'

(Matthew 24:9)

'No servant is greater than his master. If they persecuted me, they will persecute you also . . . a time is coming when anyone who kills you will think he is offering a service to God.'

(John 15:20; 16:2)

Pain, suffering and death are promised to the followers of Jesus, not worldly success, but their persecution is not without purpose.

They will lay hands on you and persecute you. They will deliver you to synagogues and prisons, and you will be brought before kings and governors, and all on account of my name. *This will result in your being witnesses to them.*

(Luke 21:12,13)

 The history of the Christian Church is littered with stories of people becoming believers when they saw how Christians met their deaths. Eternal salvation, not earthly prosperity, is our main goal.

To die, in Christ, is gain

During the evil regime of Idi Amin in Uganda, Christians were not allowed to evangelise. At a time when things were not going too well for the dictator, he ordered some public executions to try and bring in more control. Consequently three Christian men were arrested and sentenced and everyone was invited to the football stadium on a Saturday afternoon to witness them being shot.

The place was packed with every seat taken and people

standing at the back. A loud-speaker system was in place and the leader of the firing squad read out the men's names and their supposed crimes. All three of them were allowed to speak. Each of them gave their Christian testimony, preached the gospel of Jesus, and forgave their assassins, after which they were despatched to glory.

On the next day, Sunday, all the local Christian churches were packed to overflowing. The victims had gone into the nearer presence of Jesus but in the process Idi Amin had provided, free of charge, a huge stadium, a loud-speaker system, and one of the most successful evangelistic meetings ever held in Uganda.

Jesus' prophecy of two thousand years ago has proved to be amazingly accurate throughout both millenia despite its surprising content. To suggest that Christians who offer love, mercy, power and hope to all sinners will be persecuted and killed regularly in vast numbers was not a logical statement with a likely outcome. Its continuous, sad fulfilment encourages us to believe in Jesus.

Unless the unseen spiritual world is seen as the real world and death is but the gateway to eternity the problem of pain and evil in this life can be unfathomable and insurmountable. But once we have Christ, and know we have Christ, 'our present sufferings are not worth comparing with the glory that will be revealed' (Romans 8:18). Through Christ the Christian Church is granted the privilege of sharing in his sufferings, for his sake (1 Peter 4:12-13).

GROUP STUDY *The cost of discipleship*

A thoughtful question:

He is no fool who gives what he cannot keep
To gain what he cannot lose.

What does the wise man give and what does he gain?

Read John 15:18 – 16:4.

1. Why does the world oppose God the Father (John 16:3), Jesus (John 15:22,25) and Christians? (John 15:21).
2. How can we help those who do not know Jesus? (John 16:3; 15:27).
3. Who will help us to testify about Jesus? (John 15:26).
4. What may happen to those who follow Jesus? (John 15:20; 16:2).
5. In what ways might we be persecuted if we witness about Jesus?
6. Why did Jesus tell us we would be persecuted? (John 16:4).
7. If we are not being persecuted might we be doing something wrong? If so, how can we put it right?

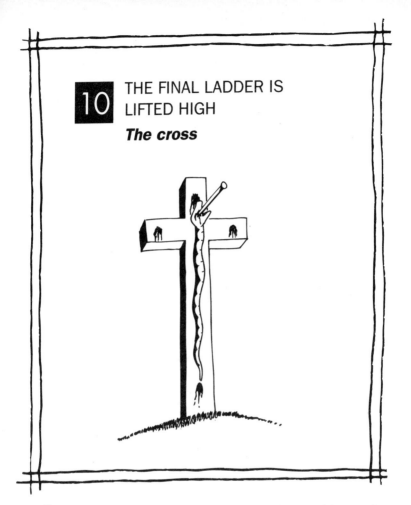

10 THE FINAL LADDER IS LIFTED HIGH

The cross

One lunch-time two teenage boys from Bridgenorth Grammar School wandered into the adjoining church. They weren't particularly looking for mischief, just something to do with an idle half-hour in the middle of the day, but once they saw what was inside the idea of a gentle sight-seeing tour gave way to the thought of something far more exciting and adventurous. There before them was a series of ladders interspersed with various platforms reaching up to a very high scaffold just below the ceiling. The men working on the roof had dispersed for their lunch-break, no one was around, and the temptation to climb high was irresistible.

Up they went, cautiously at first, until by the time the highest ladder was scaled some degree of sure-footedness and freedom was being expressed in their movements. They enjoyed a marvellous time among the rafters, clambered over anything and everything, and quickly became cheekily confident in the process. Unfortunately as they larked about they loosened one of the boards and at a moment when both of them were on one end it gave way. In see-saw fashion the loose plank angled down like a slide causing both lads to slip through helplessly in quick succession. The younger and smaller boy went down first and saved himself by hanging onto a beam while the older lad slid after him and only avoided the vertical drop by clinging onto the legs of his younger friend.

The workmen were due back any moment so the teenagers did their best to hang on. Suspended many feet above a stone floor they encouraged one another with the thought that help was only a few minutes away but sadly the men didn't return as quickly as they hoped. Gradually, as the seconds ticked by and no one came, utter exhaustion appeared on the face of the younger boy and his grip began to slacken. The older one sensed it was happening and responded almost immediately. 'If I wasn't weighing you down,' he asked his friend, 'do you think you could hold on for another ten minutes?' There was silence for a few seconds and a brief moment's hesitation before the younger boy summoned up enough energy to reply. 'Yes,' he replied in a barely audible whisper, 'I think I could.'

The older lad gave him a message for his mother, said goodbye and then let go. After what seemed like only a second or two there was a dull thud on the church floor and then everything went very quiet. Relieved of his friend's

weight the younger schoolboy hung on for a few more minutes until the echo of footsteps in an empty church broke the
deadly silence. The returning workmen rushed instantly to
the crumpled heap lying motionless on the floor but there
was nothing they could do. Falling from such a height onto a
stone floor had brought instant death. The adults weighed up
the scene in seconds and in so doing naturally looked
upwards to the place from whence the boy had fallen.
Adjusting their eyes to the gloom among the rafters they
thought they saw something moving and although the ladder
was very high the experienced and fit roofers made the ascent
speedily. They were just in time to rescue the boy from next
door and save him from following in his friend's footsteps.

The story is an old one but a true one. A straightforward
sacrifice. One dies that the other might live – freely given.
Greater love has no-one than this.

The sacrifice

After Ezra, Nehemiah, Zerubbabel and the prophet
Haggai helped the Israelites to return from Babylon,
silence reigned. There was nothing to put in the
Bible, and no one to put it there for nearly four hundred years. The Greeks came and were repelled by Judas
Maccabaeus but the Romans replaced them. King Herod was
not their king, not a Davidic king and not a very nice piece of
work. Like a malfunctioning machine Israel shut down and
attempted to recharge her batteries during the prophetic
absence. The Jews were waiting for God, deliverance featured
in everybody's dreams but no one was looking for a sacrifice.

The problem was that neither the Old Testament writers
nor the prophets understood that Messiah was coming twice.
They foresaw political peace: lions munching grass with sheep
while Israel was top-dog, but they didn't realise this was for
next time. The learned scholars of Herod's day were unable
and probably unwilling to teach scriptural exposition which

would prepare the people for a substitutionary atonement. They missed Isaiah 53, they missed the suffering servant, and they nearly missed Jesus.

Only a man whose life was kick-started by angels, who was full of the Holy Spirit from birth, who lived an ascetic, godly lifestyle, who became strong in spirit and possessed the greatest prophetic gift known to humankind – only John the Baptist spotted him. 'The next day John saw Jesus coming towards him and said, "Look, the Lamb of God, who takes away the sin of the world!"' (John 1:29).

The sacrifice had come.

Many roads lead to the cross

Jesus was the first person to ask *why* he had to die on the cross. 'My God, my God, *why* have you forsaken me?' he cried out in the midst of the barbaric torture, humiliation and anguish he suffered on Good Friday (Matthew 27:46). Like different roads which lead to the same destination the New Testament gives us more than one answer but if we put them together we see something of the glory of God displayed at Calvary. I believe God reveals the following truths to us about the cross of Christ:

1. It displays the love of God

According to the New Testament Jesus did not have his life taken from him by evil men, but chose to lay it down. Like the older boy from Bridgenorth Grammar School Jesus let go of his life for the sake of others. This truth can be found in all four Gospels but it finds its clearest expression in John. Jesus said: 'I lay down my life – only to take it up again. No-one takes it from me, but I lay it down of my own accord. I have authority to lay it down and authority to take it up again. This command I received from my Father' (John 10:17-18).

Sweating, 'like drops of blood falling to the ground' the night before he died (Luke 22:43-44), crying out from the cross in great pain with a real sense of dereliction (Matthew 27:45-50), the cross shows us something of how much Jesus loves us. He said, 'My command is this: Love each other as I have loved you. Greater love has no-one than this that he lay down his life for his friends' (John 15:12-13).

2. It highlights our sin

In the Old Testament God kept loving and forgiving his people, calling them to return to him, taking them back and starting again, but they never made it because of their sinfulness. 'All have sinned and fall short of the glory of God' (Romans 3:23). The climax of such failure is seen in the rejection of Christ. The coming to earth of God in human form to offer himself as the escalator to heaven met with wholesale humiliation and murder. The rejection of Christ is the most graphic display imaginable of the fallen condition of people made in the image of God, and their need for salvation. It is the darkest blot in human history.

Betrayed by Judas, denied by Peter, deserted by the other ten disciples, arrested by the Jewish leaders, condemned by the ordinary people who preferred the criminal Barabbas, sentenced by the Roman authorities, the suffering servant was despised and rejected as he died a cruel death on the cross. The world's sin and need for salvation is brought into the light by the darkness of the cross of Christ.

3. It reveals a participation in our sufferings

At the cross we see Jesus' love for us highlighted against the very dark backdrop of our own failure, but the victims of other people's sins see in Christ a fellow-traveller – a participator in their sufferings, and one who can share in their pain.

Whenever I try to help someone who has been physically or sexually abused I always bring them to the cross to meet Jesus before I can offer him to them as the healer. The discovery that the head of the Christian Church is an abused victim is nearly always a helpful revelation.

4. It offers a new relationship with God

The Bible uses several metaphors to explain the new relationship with God which can become ours through the cross.

There is the commercial metaphor – *redemption* – God pays the price to buy back what originally belonged to him (Ephesians 1:7). Christ's death frees us from bondage to the four tyrants of wrath, sin, law and death (Romans 5,6,7,8).

There is the political metaphor – *reconciliation* – when two alienated parties make peace. God's purpose of love was to reconcile the world to himself (Colossians 1:19-20).

There is the legal metaphor – *justification* – allowing the guilty to be declared innocent and forgiveness to become a moral option as the price is paid. Justice is satisfied but love triumphs as Jesus fulfils the law (Romans 3:23-26). Sinners who repent and believe in Jesus, receive Jesus' death as a substitute for their own and are now forgiven.

There is the captivity metaphor – *ransom* – the price paid for the release of a prisoner (Mark 10:45).

There is the battle metaphor – *salvation* – delivered from the enemy of judgement, the consequences of sin, to the hope of resurrection. Saved from death to life and, of course, there has to be a death if there is to be a rising from the dead (Acts 4:10-12).

Although the previous five metaphors are all biblical, the Bible majors on the religious metaphor – a *sacrifice* (Romans 3:25). The lamb of God who takes away the sin of the world, dies at Passover. Jesus explains at the Last Supper how he is giving his life for the forgiveness of sins. Isaiah sees the death of the suffering servant as a sinless 'guilt-offering', and the writer to the Hebrews informs us that Jesus' sacrifice ends all sacrifices, making it possible for believers to receive the death of Christ by faith, enter the holy of holies and come into God's presence (Hebrews 10:10-14).

5. *It conquers Satan* – Christus victor

On the night before he died Jesus took bread and wine as symbols of his body and blood representing the new covenant which his death on the cross initiated. Whenever we *celebrate* Holy Communion by eating bread and drinking wine publicly in remembrance of Jesus we proclaim his death until he comes again, and we proclaim it as a *victory*.

Christ's victory in the New Testament is seen as the conquering of Satan, robbing him of his greatest weapon, death. Consider these verses:

> The reason the Son of God appeared was to destroy the devil's work. (1 John 3:8)
>
> The prince of this world now stands condemned. (John 16:11)
>
> Having disarmed the powers and authorities, he made a public spectacle of them, triumphing over them by the cross. (Colossians 2:15)
>
> By his death he destroyed him who holds the power of death – that is the devil – and freed those who all their lives were held in slavery by their fear of death. (Hebrews 2:14)

The Son of Mary has crushed the serpent's head as Jesus cries out in triumph from the cross, 'It is finished' (John 19:30). God's justice replaces Satan's punishment and people are now free to move legally from under Satan's headship to Jesus' Lordship.

Quite how Jesus defeated Satan at the cross is not made absolutely clear in Scripture but that Christ's work was a mighty victory is a vital truth. Those who belong to Christ are on the winning side. Jesus was able to say to the believing, penitent thief who died with him, 'Today you will be with me in paradise' (Luke 23:43). The thief became the first-fruit of many who once belonged to Satan but now belong to Christ.

I believe all these roads meet at the cross and explain

something of God's purposes. Jesus' death reveals how much God loves us but also how much we have sinned; Jesus identifies with our sufferings yet offers himself as a sacrifice for us; he has paid the price, he has overcome Satan, he can and does offer forgiveness without compromising justice and he is the only one who can bring us to the Father. The cross of Christ says 'yes' to all these biblical ideas which come together at Golgotha.

The cross for the outsider

We find these important truths in the Bible with others besides and yet . . . for over twenty years, despite such understanding, I struggled to know what to say to the outsider about Good Friday. At times all the various ideas and theories seemed a bit too clever and out of reach for those who didn't come to church.

As so often happens the answer came to me while I was doing something else; while I was reading a cricket book given to me for my birthday. In it the coach died suddenly and the next day his devoted student made a century, hoping his mentor would be sitting on a fluffy cloud applauding him as he entered the pavilion.

OK! Maybe, maybe not. No information was given about the teacher's religious beliefs, but then the next day I turned on the radio hoping to hear the golf, tennis and football results and found myself listening to the end of a horse race. Lo and behold! the trainer of the winning horse died suddenly the day before and the commentator was sure he'd be sitting on another fluffy cloud, (or maybe the same one), applauding the winner into the enclosure. Now obviously there is going to be cricket in heaven – but horse racing? Another reason why Christ died on a cross suddenly dawned on me and I knew where to turn for confirmation. 'But I, when I am lifted up from the earth, will draw all men to myself. He said this to show the kind of death he was going to die' (John 12:32-33).

When Jesus was lifted up on the cross the kind of death he died drew the attention of all who saw it. The embarrasingly public nature of Jesus' humiliation soon had people from all over the earth talking about it and the excruciatingly painful experience he suffered has shocked the world ever since. It clangs across the globe like a loud alarm-bell in a blazing factory and most people come to hear it at some stage in their lifetime. The awfulness of the event does not require a knowledge of Jewish history or a degree in theology to interpret its simple message: God would not be shouting so loudly to the whole world from the hill of Calvary unless he required a response that really mattered. God is offering his Son for our salvation in such a way that we are left with no excuse for ignoring him or rejecting him.

If we think playing cricket or going to the races will get us into heaven while we fail to respond to the bloody death of God then I suggest we need to *pause for thought*. This is how John preached the cross in his Gospel.

Like a ladder reaching from the earth into the heavens the cross was silhouetted against the dark sky, high on a hill. The man who claimed to be God was nailed to it for all to see. On the cross the title 'King of the Jews', 'was written in Aramaic, Latin and Greek' (John 19:20). The Davidic king was announced publicly to the whole world in the language of the Roman Empire, the language of the Greek Empire, and the language of the Middle East. The King of the Jews was proclaimed as the universal Christ.

Jesus was not killed quietly and quickly in a corner but publicly and painfully over several hours. Most of the theories of the atonement would still work if Jesus had been killed by Herod the Great as a baby, but the world, needing to see and believe in order to obtain eternal life, was not going to be given the chance of missing this event. If it was just his death that mattered then being stoned like Stephen or dying of a heart attack in Gethsemane would have been fine, but when they did try to stone him Jesus' hour had not yet come. The timing, the publicity, the visibility and the horror of this moment were far too important for it to be hushed up in a secret place. When Christ died it was important the world should know about it.

Today the prophecy of Jesus, recorded in John, of focussing the eyes of the whole world on the manner of his death is being fulfilled all over the planet. The cross stands out on the top of every Christian church as a horrific symbol of execution; we wear them round our necks and in our lapels, we put them on our Bibles and in our cemeteries; they are splattered across the world for all to see and to the man or woman in the street or on the golf course who likes to think everybody is going to heaven they cry out, 'NO! A thousand times NO! You are not OK. God would not come to earth, be lifted up in torment, naked and blood-stained, for the whole earth to see if you were already OK; if it didn't matter.' The crucifixion of Christ is there to grab our attention. Whatever Calvary means, it means that God would not have done it this way if it hadn't been necessary; Jesus would not have died so obviously in such anguish if you and I were going to be OK any way. God cries out from his high wooden tower to the whole world, 'You are not OK and never will be OK unless you accept my Son as your Saviour.'

 The cross of Christ is not intended merely to be discussed over coffee in the university common room. It is meant to be taken into the world, out on the streets, and lifted up high in order to declare God's message: 'This is for you, it's free, it is the gateway to life, it is the ladder to heaven – but – ignore it at your peril.' It's not what we do on the cricket-pitch or the racecourse that gets us into heaven but how we respond to what Jesus has done for us.

Accepting Jesus

'He was in the world, and though the world was made through him, the world did not recognise him. He came to that which was his own, but his own did not receive him' (John 1:10-11).

'Yet,' says John, 'to all who received him, to those who believed in his name, he gave the right to become children of God' (John 1:12).

There were some wise men from the East, probably from Iraq like Abraham, who recognised Jesus, received him, believed in his name and worshipped him. There were some Jewish shepherds, outcasts because they looked after the Temple sheep on the Sabbath, who with the help of some brightly adorned night visitors recognised Jesus, received him and believed in his name. There was a fisherman who tried to kill a man with a sword, a Samaritan woman living in sin having worked her way through five husbands; an influential Pharisee, a rich gardener, a little children's playgroup, a deceitful tax-collector, a Roman centurion, a wild, naked man in a cemetery, all kinds of sick, diseased, unclean people, several beggars, a prostitute or two, a dying thief, three dead people and eventually his mother, brothers and a university professor.

Whoever! Whoever recognises Jesus, receives him and believes in his name become children of God and inherit eternal life. This is why Christ died publicly, painfully on a cross for all to see.

'And as Moses lifted up the serpent in the wilderness, so must the Son of Man be lifted up, that *whoever* believes in him may have eternal life' (John 3:14-15, RSV).

The eleventh hour

When I went to Christ Church, Ward End as Vicar in 1979

Harold Jones was one of the few men who attended our over-sixties club on a Thursday. His father had been a talented pub pianist and as he could busk along himself quite adequately Harold was much in demand by the ladies for their regular singalongs.

Harold rarely ever came to church services. His father was a Christadelphian elder who went off with another woman leaving his mum to bring up five children on her own. Two of them died and the others endured the poverty and hardship which hit so many people between the two world wars. Organised religion and Harold never seemed to fit comfortably together after that.

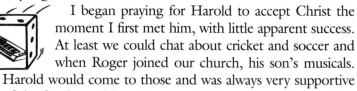 I began praying for Harold to accept Christ the moment I first met him, with little apparent success. At least we could chat about cricket and soccer and when Roger joined our church, his son's musicals. Harold would come to those and was always very supportive of the family, enabling Roger and Mary to attend a number of Christian meetings by offering his talented and popular baby-sitting services, but getting him to church on a Sunday proved beyond us.

My hopes of helping Harold to make a commitment to Christ took a downward slide when Roger left teaching for Christian music ministry and I took some of the blame. Afterwards our relationship was polite and I tried to keep in touch but he never came back to the over sixties club. In 1982 Roger and Mary were in Germany while Roger's dad had an operation on his bladder so I visited him in hospital and was able to ring them with the good news that it was only warts and they'd been scraped away successfully.

In 1983 he needed further treatment and nurse Mary soon realised it was cancer of the bladder. Radiotherapy managed to prolong his life but from then on there was constant discomfort which eventually gave way to distress and pain. I visited him several times in hospital and he always expressed deep gratitude to the nurses for all they did for him, and for Mary.

In 1986 Harold moved to Roger and Mary's house and into Tim's room, while Tim at the age of eleven made do on a collapsible bed in his parents' room. It was then that I realised a new opportunity was presenting itself for Roger's dad to find Christ before he died. He'd always thought the world of Mary. 'Now that's a real Christian,' he often used to say to me. It dawned on me that 'incarnation' was perhaps the only real way of communicating the gospel left to us in this situation.

When Christ was on earth people became believers by saying, 'yes,' to the person of Jesus. It wasn't a system of words, formulas, saying particular prayers or signing cards but a real relationship with a fully human being. Today Jesus is not here in the flesh but those who have accepted Christ have the Spirit of Christ living in them. Christians are the body of Christ. As Mary was loving and caring towards Harold she was being Christ to him and he was very definitely saying, 'yes,' to the Christ within Mary. 'He who receives you,' says Jesus, 'receives me' (Matthew 10:40).

Seeing this enabled me to pray differently. Harold was uncomfortable with organised religion because of his father's misdeeds, but the person of Jesus Christ was a different matter; he'd always enjoyed Roger's musicals which presented the character of Jesus in dramatic form. I began to pray not for Harold to come to church, not even for him to read a book, say a prayer or sign a card, but whatever it might mean I prayed for him to say, 'yes,' to Jesus. He'd already recognised Jesus in Mary and now he needed to receive Jesus and believe in his name.

Mary nursed Harold while Roger, Mary, many friends and I prayed for him every day. Mary is normally shy and quiet, hates the limelight and ninety-nine per cent of the time likes to get on with life in an efficient, ordinary kind of way. But just occasionally, one per cent of the time, when she believes something strongly and feels it deeply, she can be formidable;

like Boadicea riding to battle in her chariot.

When 'Pop', as she called Roger's dad, began to deteriorate she spoke frankly to him. 'Not too good today Pop,' she said. 'I think it's time to make your peace with God, don't you?' He agreed. He didn't know much about the different denominations but he did know Mary was a real Christian. In his own way, in his own words, he did the business with God through Jesus.

Mary checked up on him some time later. 'Have you done it then?' she enquired. 'Made your peace with God?' Simply but sincerely he admitted he had.

Harold went into hospital soon after that and died a few days later. I took the funeral believing him to be with Jesus. Pam Griffiths sang, 'When I survey the wondrous cross,' and Roger felt able to accompany her. It was very moving. The setting was from Roger's *Saints Alive*, which was Harold's favourite musical.

The prince of glory died on the wondrous cross for the Harolds of this world as well as for bishops and popes. Only God, by his Holy Spirit, can convict and convert, which is why prayer is so important, but I believe it is the responsibili-

ty of all Christian churches and every born-again believer to make this good news known. The cross of Christ is meant for everyone.

A prayer for becoming a Christian

Lord Jesus, thank you for dying for me on the cross. I repent of my sins and ask you to come into my life by your Holy Spirit to be my Lord and Saviour. Amen.

GROUP STUDY *The cross*

An important question: If you died tonight how would you stand before the judgement throne of God?

Read John 19:16-31.

1. Noah was universally significant. In what way was the cucifixion of Jesus, as described in John, seen to be universally significant? (John 19:20).
2. How was the death of Christ like an incident in Abraham's life? (Genesis 22).
3. At the first Passover, Moses was told to kill a lamb, which was subsequently done on the day of preparation. He took a bunch of hyssop, dipped it in the lamb's blood and put some on the door-frame. Afterwards, at Passover celebrations, they drank four cups of red wine. The fourth cup was the cup of completion sometimes drunk to the toast, 'It is finished.' How many of these Passover activities can you find in John's account of the crucifixion? Why did John include them?
4. Why did Pilate say, 'What I have written, I have written'? (John 19:22). How did it fulfil God's covenant promise to David?
5. How many Old Testament prophecies does John see being fulfilled at Golgotha? (John 19:24,28,36,37).
6. Where did the suffering servant's spirit go when he died? (John 19:30).
7. Where will your spirit go when you die?

NO SERPENTS IN HEAVEN
A new creation

One day as I was lying on my bed and praying with my eyes closed, I saw a picture of a dark and gloomy world. At first I thought I was visiting a slate mine in Wales but then I realised it was a more normal environment only without colour. The houses were grey, the streets were grey, the clouds above were black and grey, and everywhere I looked the bowed, Lowry-type figures were also grey.

My mood grew darker and I felt very sad. I scanned every

home, street and face but could find no light and no vibrancy anywhere. The daily round of trudgery and drudgery had engulfed them all and I longed to escape to a better place. 'Is there no hope?' I asked God in my prayers. 'Is there no way out?'

'Keep looking,' he seemed to say.

I looked and found nothing to dispel the immediate drabness but after a period of intense concentration I spotted a glimmer of hope on the distant horizon in the middle of a dark, high, endless wall. As I followed it round with my eyes I discovered how the whole of this grey existence was walled in at its outer perimeters, and only in one tiny spot was there a ray of brightness sneaking through.

The pin-point of light drew me like a magnet and as I made my way towards it I saw myself in the picture for the first time, grey like everyone else. It felt very strange, almost eerie, that no one else was aware of the light and no one was noticing me. Perhaps they were too busy with the 'oughtages' and 'mustages' of the daily round.

When I arrived at the source of the illumination I was taken completely by surprise. It was not what I expected to find. There in the wall, about the height of a man, was a gap which went down to the ground, made in the shape of a cross. The luminosity was too great to see to the other side, outside the city wall, but I knew I wanted to go through.

I struggled for a while to make the transition from this world into the next-door one until it dawned on me that the only way I could penetrate the hole was to make myself into the shape of a cross. With arms outstretched it was still a tight squeeze but by breathing in I fitted like the last piece of a jigsaw puzzle and shuffled through into a whole new experience.

My eyes took a while adjusting to the glare but in due course they feasted on an incredible, multi-coloured world. The grass was emerald green like a child's painting and the sparkling stream which flowed through the land was the deep, pure blue of a sapphire. Bright birds of every shade and hue darted about singing joyfully while young animals jostled playfully across the whole pageant. I took some steps, breathed in the freshness, and felt more at home than being at home. I was attracted to a park bench close to the water where a man in white was seated and as I took my place beside him he turned and smiled.

I've never seen such a warm, gentle, compassionate look in a person's eyes, which at the same time was so strong and full of wisdom. It was as if he knew me; knew all about me and yet loved me and accepted me in a way I'd never experienced in the monochrome world.

'Hello Peter,' he said kindly. 'Welcome.'

'You're not. . .?' I began hesitantly.

'Oh no,' he responded quickly, knowingly. 'When you see him you won't be going back. Come, let me show you a few sights.'

Although the world and its sights were dazzling, being with him was the number one experience for me. 'If only he'd taught me French at school,' I thought to myself, 'maybe I'd have passed'.

As we walked along, an unexpected sight came across our path – a man in a wheelchair. My friend approached him gently. 'Didn't you know,' he asked quietly, 'that you can walk in this world?' The man could hardly believe it but he allowed the white figure to help him up; slowly at first but then with greater freedom and joy as he stumbled, walked, ran and eventually leapt into the air. We came across another person in a wheelchair and my friend said I could try it. The thrill of helping him up and seeing him take his first steps outmatched anything and everything from the old grey world.

We arrived at a funfair and my companion communicated to me silently with an informed look. Since birth I have suffered from motion sickness and was never able to do a forward roll at school without getting a headache. The thought of travelling in a car made me queasy and as a child I was always sick whenever I did.

'Shall we?' he asked. Like the men in the wheelchairs I'd never have dared try it on my own but with him beside me even the big dipper was sensational.

Afterwards it took a little while to realise our ramblings were now taking us back towards the hole in the wall. As we drew nearer I noticed the cross was much bigger in colour than it had been in black and white, and a force coming from it began to suck me in.

'Can't I stay here?' I asked as my feet began to lose their grip.

'Not now,' said the man in white. 'You still have work to do. Take some light from this world to those who dwell in darkness. Don't be afraid. He'll be with you, by his Spirit.'

I wanted to ask why they didn't brick up the hole in the wall but as I was pulled through I knew it needed to stay open for others.

It wasn't real. It wasn't Scripture. It was only a picture. 'No eye has seen, no ear has heard, no mind has conceived what God has prepared for those who love him' (1 Corinthians 2:9). And yet, it has stayed with me since then and at times helped me to understand unseen reality.

The Spirit comes

The cross on its own was not sufficient to convince the world of Jesus' claims and few would have remained his followers if he'd stayed in the tomb.

It was Jesus' resurrection appearances that helped them to believe and understand the necessity of the cross (Luke 24:25-26); it was Jesus' ascension which gave them great joy as he assumed his rightful place in heaven (Luke 24:51-52); and it was the power of the Holy Spirit whom Jesus sent on the day of Pentecost, which enabled them to take the gospel to all nations (Acts 1:8; 2:33). Jesus hinted at it all beforehand in a prophecy.

But I tell you the truth: It is for your good that I am going away. Unless I go away, the Counsellor will not come to you; but if I go, I will send him to you. When he comes, he will convict the world of guilt in regard to sin and righteousness and judgement: in regard to sin, because men do not believe in me; in regard to righteousness, because I am going to the Father, where you can see me no longer; and in regard to judgement, because the prince of this world now stands condemned.

(John 16:7-11)

The people of Jesus' day were not prepared to believe what they thought were 'blasphemous' claims purely on the strength of the miracles Jesus did, but when 'more than five hundred' saw him alive (1 Corinthians 15:6), 'three thousand' witnessed the outpouring of the Holy Spirit at Pentecost' (Acts 2:41), and another two thousand experienced Peter healing 'a man crippled from birth . . . in the name of Jesus Christ of Nazareth', then they believed (Acts 3:2,6,7; 4:4). The guilt of the cross plus the witness of the Spirit convicted them of sin, helped them to repent and to make a commitment to Christ. Then they were filled with the Holy Spirit themselves (Acts 2:38,39) and he affirmed them as children of God (Galatians 4:6-7).

 Jesus told his disciples to ask their heavenly Father to send the Holy Spirit, again and again, and promised them he would always do so (Luke 11:13). He would not send them a snake but rather their authority in Jesus would enable them to 'trample on snakes' (Luke 11:11; 10:19). The continued work of the Spirit in the lives of the believers demonstrated this authority they now had over Satan, the prince of this world. Becoming a Christian was seen as turning 'from darkness to light, and from the power of Satan to God' (Acts 26:18); healing was seen as releasing people 'who were under the power of the devil', even those bitten by snakes (Acts

10:38; 28:3-6); and deliverance was understood as the evict-
ing of 'evil spirits' (Acts 8:7). The whole process was so new
and so transforming that Paul described being a Christian as
having become a new creation: 'If anyone is in Christ, he is a
new creation; the old has gone, the new has come' (2
Corinthians 5:17).

It could be seen as bringing the technicolour of God's
kingdom into the darkness and drabness of Satan's dominion
– in the power of the Holy Spirit – all made possible through
the cross of Christ. The Holy Spirit gives us a foretaste of
heaven here on earth. There is continual worship in heaven
and he helps us now to become true worshippers. There is no
pain and suffering in heaven and he brings healing to spirit,
soul and body. There are no serpents in heaven and he
empowers us to cast out demons and to wrestle with princi-
palities and powers in this present age.

Wholeness through Christ

Roger's mum died in 1975 following forty-four
years of happy marriage, at the age of sixty-five.
After she had been ill for some time the medical
profession diagnosed lung cancer in January and
she died in June.

Winifred was a good mum who did everything for Roger;
in fact too much. Given the circumstances of Roger's birth
and being an only child this was hardly surprising, but at
times the over-protection became somewhat over-bearing.
Roger was not allowed to play football in case he was hurt
and he was not permitted to take the eleven-plus examination
in case he failed. Of course sometimes this fosters a rebellious,
stubborn-like determination which is not altogether bad. I
played cricket quite a few times with Roger in our youth and
he was one of the most fearless, dogged defenders against
genuinely fast bowling I had the pleasure to partner at the
crease. He rarely knocked the ball off the square but the

opposition rarely knocked his castle over.

The other problem, the main one, which Roger experienced with his mum went back to his birth. Separated from her for several months from the beginning there was an absence of bonding which showed itself in a lack of emotional attachment to her. Roger and his mum always behaved well towards one another but Roger 'felt' very little and consequently at her death, assured somewhat by her Anglo-Catholic faith, there were no tears. There was genuine sadness that she had gone but life carried on in much the same emotionless way as before. Roger knew he was burying his feelings and pushing the bereavement down but despite prayers he felt powerless to do anything about it. It is not easy nor necessarily appropriate to make oneself cry just because others suggest it ought to be so.

The positive thing about not feeling emotionally whole was that Roger realised there was a problem and consequently he was always keen to hear people like John Wimber, Mary Pytches or Dr Chris Andrew teach on the subject of healing, whenever he could. So often God turns our weaknesses into his opportunities and this openness assisted him in learning much about wholeness and becoming sensitive to others with emotional difficulties.

The breakthrough for Roger, personally, came when he attended a 'Wholeness Through Christ' conference. The leaders gave a good chunk of solid biblical teaching then saw each person individually for a session while everyone else prayed. Although there was much room for individuality, spontaneity and the guidance of the Holy Spirit they systematically worked through the four areas which identify their particular approach to healing. In diagrammatic form they were presented as four quadrants of a circle.

1. *Sins* – Wholeness through Christ as opposed to wholeness through science or medicine naturally begins with being right with God and one another through Jesus. Our own sins cut

us off from God and damage our relationships with others. We need to confess, repent and renounce these and receive forgiveness from God through Christ and other Christians. Often, especially for mature Christians, it is not just deliberate sin that affects us but wrong thinking and reactions. On this occasion Roger sensed God wanted him to repent for failing to forgive Mum and Dad for not being there in the first few months of his life, which he did gladly.

2. *Wounds* – Sometimes when people or circumstances have hurt us we forgive them but the emotional scars remain. When we have not been hugged we still have not been hugged after we have forgiven our non-tactile or absent relatives. The Christian can then pray for God, through Jesus, to come and give the person those hugs in the Spirit that they never had, and heal the scars. Although Roger's mum died some time ago, the Wholeness-Through-Christ counsellors prayed for Roger, in the power of the Holy Spirit with the laying-on-of hands, to receive the bonding he missed from her as a new- born baby. With eyes closed Roger saw a picture of Mum hugging him as a baby in his mind while feeling warmth and affirmation in his emotions.

3. *Bondages* – The Bible tells us that the sins of the fathers can be visited on the children to the third and fourth generations. We have seen quite a bit of this in our brief walk through the Old Testament. It is a problem area and one that not everyone finds easy to accept but experience shows that demons can pass on down the family tree when sin remains unconfessed. Then, as with Nehemiah and Daniel, we need to confess the sins of our ancestors. 'To confess' means 'to see it the same way as God sees it', so we can still confess even if we have not committed such sins ourselves. Those praying for Roger sensed God might be saying there was a generational curse of murder coming through the male line. 'Words of knowledge' are always difficult to verify, and we need to be

very careful not to put ideas into people's minds, but when prayer is going on at the same time and care is taken to suggest them in a humble way, they can be very helpful. There were some reasons for accepting the possibility of this 'word' as Roger could remember hearing of boys who had died prematurely in every recent generation of his family. When the counsellors broke this curse in Jesus' name it felt to Roger like a volcano erupting inside him.

4. *Demons* – There is no shortage of demons in the New Testament. If we can believe in God, who is Spirit, and in human beings having a spirit which survives death, then it is no more difficult to believe in the existence of other spirits, be they holy angels, unholy angels or demons. Jesus certainly believed in their existence and they certainly believed in his. The eruption in Roger felt like tension coming out of the stomach and rising up into his throat. As those praying told the demons to go in the name of Jesus there was considerable coughing until inner peace came and physical tears flowed. Roger wept for some time for the death of his mother and their lack of emotional bonding, and then felt much better; almost like a new creation.

Such an experience authenticates Scripture, builds faith and equips us to share the gospel more positively. As the Holy Spirit brings healing into various areas of our lives it helps us to become more effective in living for Christ, having faith in Christ and witnessing to Christ. When we do this we bring more of the kingdom of Christ on earth as in heaven, more light into the darkness, and create an alternative society in full colour that is more likely to attract other people. Primarily the work of the Spirit today helps people to know Christ and to make him known so that they may be ready for the next-door world. The Holy Spirit prepares new creations for the new creation.

When the time arrives for Christians to end their present existence on this earth there is a ladder waiting for them.

Symbolically Jesus is that ladder, the gate to heaven and the way to the Father. Angels ascend and descend on the ladder and when our hour has come the stairway may work either up or down for us.

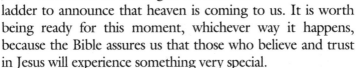

Either we will die and the angels will take us up the ladder and into heaven or else Jesus will return as the angels descend the ladder to announce that heaven is coming to us. It is worth being ready for this moment, whichever way it happens, because the Bible assures us that those who believe and trust in Jesus will experience something very special.

In the age to come there are features and godly activities which will no longer be needed or relevant such as tears, witnessing or deliverance. There are, however, many other ideas, significant people's names, themes and topics running throughout Scripture which are highlighted in what is to come. Notice how many of them are pictured coming together like a new world symphony at the end of this present age. (The following description of the place Jesus has prepared for his followers is adapted from the book of Revelation; Isaiah 49, 54, 65; Daniel 7 and Joel 3.)

A new world symphony

There will be a new heaven and a new earth shining with the glory of God like clear crystal. The river of the water of life will be flowing through the land and all who are thirsty will drink without cost. The mountains will drip new wine, the hills will flow with milk and the lion will lie down with the lamb. The new city will be built with stones of turquoise, its foundations with sapphires and the streets paved with pure gold like transparent glass.

The creator who makes all things new will be present in the new Jerusalem where we shall see him face to face. John saw him dressed in a robe as white as snow reaching down to his feet with a golden sash round his chest. The hair of his head was white like wool, his eyes ablaze, his feet like bronze glowing in a furnace with a river of fire coming out from before him. In his hand he held seven stars and his face was like the sun shining in all its brilliance.

In glory Jesus helps us to understand his pre-existence and his sovereignty. Jesus says to us: 'I am the Alpha and the Omega, the First and the Last, the Beginning and the End ... I was dead, and behold I am alive for ever and ever ... I am ... the bright morning star' (Revelation 22:13,16; 1:18).

The new creation is prepared for God who is Spirit, angels who are ministering spirits, and people made in the image of God whose spirits have been born again. John saw thousands upon thousands of angels, and ten thousand times ten thousand circling around the throne. Seven of them had been entrusted with the great and marvellous sign of the last seven plagues with which they defeated the beast. They had harps and sang the song of Moses: 'Great and marvellous are your deeds, Lord God Almighty. Just and true are your ways, King of the ages' (Revelation 15:3).

People who repent, who believe in Jesus, who have their names written in his book of life and on the palms of his hands, and who wash their robes in his blood shed at the cross, will worship him. They will see God's temple revealing the ark of his covenant inside. At this time there will be flashes of lightning, rumblings, peals of thunder, an earthquake and a hailstorm and the prayers of the saints will be received by God. After this they will not need the light of a lamp nor sunlight, nor a temple any more for the Lord God will be with them and be their light.

Those who refuse to repent, including the devil himself, will be judged and not allowed to enter the city of God. There are no serpents in heaven.

The suffering servants, who have obeyed God's commandments and held to the testimony of Jesus and the word of God, will come out of the great tribulation and see Jesus as the lamb who was slain; he will wipe away every tear from their eyes and comfort them like a shepherd.

Many children of Abraham will be standing before the throne from every nation, tribe, people and language. They will taste the fruit from the tree of life and reap the benefit of its leaves which are for the healing of the nations. They will see Noah's rainbow encircling the throne on which will be seated the lion of the tribe of Judah, the root and the offspring of David. On his head will be many crowns and on his robe this name will be written: KING OF KINGS AND LORD OF LORDS.

God will dwell with his people and be their God. There will be no more death, or mourning, or pain. The sound of weeping and of crying will be heard no more, and all believers will reign with God for ever and ever.

The prophets will receive their reward and rejoice in God's victory over all evil. The bride of Christ, the Christian Church, will also be celebrating.

Let us rejoice and be glad and give him glory! For the wedding of the Lamb has come, and his bride has made herself ready. . .Blessed are those who are invited to the wedding supper of the Lamb!

(Revelation 19:7,9)

In the new creation under the rainbow at the top of Jacob's ladder those who love Jesus will be having a party to which everyone is invited. 'The Spirit and the bride say "Come!" And let him who hears say, "Come". Whoever is thirsty, let him come; and whoever wishes, let him take the free gift of the water of life' (Revelation 22:17).

Once the angels have taken us up the ladder into heaven or the New Creation has come down from heaven to earth with the return of Jesus, then the game of biblical Snakes and Ladders will be over. It is not like the ordinary board game which can only have one winner because everyone who accepts the Spirit's invitation by believing in Jesus wins and inherits a crown of glory. Life is not a race where we seek to beat everybody; life is a journey where our aim is to walk with one another, to help one another, to love one another and thereby arrive at our destination together. The greatest party of all time will be going on in heaven and I hope to see you there.

GROUP STUDY *A new creation*

 A subtle question: What was the difference between the raising of Lazarus and the raising of Jesus?
Read John 21:15-25.

1. What is the significance of Jesus asking Peter if he loved him *three times*?
2. Why was Peter hurt? (John 21:17).
3. Why did Jesus hurt Peter? (John 21:17).
4. How did Jesus reinstate Peter?
5. Who else was present whom Jesus had reinstated? (John 21:1-2). How had Jesus done that? (John 20:24-30).
6. What responsibility do we have towards others and what responsibility do we not have when following Jesus? (John 21:20-23).
7. Did Jesus help Peter to face pain or to escape from pain? How might he do the same for us?

FIFTEEN 'I AM'S IN JOHN'S GOSPEL

1. Then Jesus declared. '*I AM* the bread of life. He who comes to me will never go hungry' (John 6:35).
2. When Jesus spoke again to the people, he said, '*I AM* the light of the world. Whoever follows me will never walk in darkness, but will have the light of life' (John 8:12).
3. Therefore Jesus said again . . . '*I AM* the gate; whoever enters through me will be saved' (John 10:7,9).
4. *I AM* the good shepherd. The good shepherd lays down his life for the sheep (John 10:11).
5. Jesus said to her, '*I AM* the resurrection and the life. He who believes in me will live, even though he dies; and whoever lives and believes in me will never die' (John 11:25-26).
6. Jesus answered, '*I AM* the way and the truth and the life. No one comes to the Father except through me' (John 14:6).
7. *I AM* the true vine . . . you are the branches. If a man remains in me and I in him, he will bear much fruit; apart from me you can do nothing (John 15: 1,5).
8. In John 4 Jesus talks to the woman at the well and in verses 25 and 26 the identity of Jesus is discussed. This is how verse 26 appears in the Greek. 'Jesus: I AM *(EGO EIMI)* – the one – speaking – to you.'

In other words: 'Jesus said: I AM *(EGO EIMI)* is the one speaking to you.'

9. In John 6 Jesus came to the disciples walking on the water. 'But he said to them: I AM *(EGO EIMI)*; don't be afraid' (John 6:19).

From verse 12 onwards John 8 is all about the identity of Jesus and contains four 'I AM's.

10. The Greek at the beginning of verse 18 appears like this.

'I AM *(EGO EIMI)* – the one – witnessing – concerning – myself.'

11. In the NIV version the 'I AM' of verse 24 can be seen clearly, remembering that the words included in brackets by the translators are not in the original Greek.

'If you do not believe that I AM, *(EGO EIMI)*, you will indeed die in your sins' (John 8:24).

12. The same is true in verse 28, NIV.

So Jesus said, 'When you have lifted up the Son of Man, then you will know that I AM' *(EGO EIMI)*.

13. At the end of chapter eight Jesus' response to his interrogators is not grammatically correct unless 'I AM' is a title.

'"I tell you the truth" Jesus answered, "before Abraham was born, I AM!" *(EGO EIMI)*. At this they picked up stones to stone him' (John 8:58-59).

The Jews who were present knew what Jesus was claiming.

14. In John 13 Jesus says these words prior to informing his disciples about his betrayal: 'I am telling you now before it happens, so that when it does happen you will believe that I AM' *(EGO EIMI)* (John 13:19).

15. In John 18 Judas Iscariot, the betrayer, came with soldiers and officials from the chief priests and Pharisees to arrest him. John records this: 'When Jesus said, *"EGO EIMI"*, they drew back and fell to the ground' (John 18:6).

It is also interesting to note that the last chapter of the Bible includes a sixteenth 'I AM'.

Jesus says, 'I am the Alpha and the Omega, the First and the Last, the Beginning and the End' (Revelation 22:13). On this occasion, however, *'EIMI'* is not in the Greek text and we cannot claim the title 'I AM'.

SOME 'ONE ANOTHER'S FROM THE NEW TESTAMENT (NOT ALL ARE FROM THE NIV)

Mark 9:50	Be at peace with one another. (RSV)
John 13:14	You also should wash one another's feet.
John 13:34	Love one another. (Eleven times in the New Testament)
Romans 12:5	So all of us, united with Christ, form one body, serving individually as limbs and organs to one another. (NEB)
Romans 12:16	Live in harmony with one another.
Romans 15:7	Accept one another.
Romans 15:14	Instruct one another.
Romans 16:16	Greet one another.
1 Corinthians 11:33	Wait for one another. (RSV)
1 Corinthians 12:25	Have the same care for one another. (RSV)
Galatians 5:13	Serve one another in love.
Galatians 6:2	Bear one another's burdens. (RSV)
Ephesians 4:2	Be patient, bearing with one another in love.
Colossians 3:13	Forbearing one another and forgiving one another. (KJV)
1 Thessalonians 3:12	May the Lord make your love mount and overflow for one another. (NEB)
1 Thessalonians 4:18	Comfort one another. (RSV)

Hebrews 10:24	Let us consider how we may spur one another on towards love and good deeds.
James 4:11	Do not slander one another.
James 5:9	Don't grumble . . . against one another.
James 5:16	Confess your sins to one another, and pray for one another that you may be healed. (RSV)
1 Peter 1:22	Love one another deeply, from the heart.
1 Peter 4:9	Offer hospitality to one another without grumbling.
1 Peter 5:5	Clothe yourselves with humility towards one another.
1 John 1:7	Have fellowship with one another.

JUST AS MOSES – THE EXODUS MOTIF IN THE NEW TESTAMENT

Just as Moses was saved from being murdered as a baby by Pharoah so Jesus is saved from being murdered as a baby by Herod (Matthew 2:13-20).

Just as Moses spent forty years in the wilderness so Jesus spent forty days in the wilderness but without sin (Luke 4:1-13).

Just as Moses 'gave them bread from heaven to eat' so Jesus fed five thousand with 'five small barley loaves and two small fish' (John 6:1-3). But the teaching which accompanies this miracle puts Jesus on another plane. ' "For the bread of God is he who comes down from heaven and gives life to the world . . . Jesus declared, "I am the bread of life. He who comes to me will never go hungry"' (John 6:33,35).

Just as Moses provided water for the community by striking the rock (Numbers 20:11) so Jesus said, 'If anyone is thirsty, let him come to me and drink' (John 7:37). Paul writes:

> For I do not want you to be ignorant of the fact, brothers, that our forefathers were all under the cloud and that they all passed through the sea. They were all baptised into Moses in the cloud and in the sea. They all ate the same spiritual food and drank from the same spiritual drink; for they drank from the spiritual rock that accompanied them, and that rock was Christ.
>
> (1 Corinthians 10:1-4)

Just as God led Moses 'in a pillar of fire to give them light' (Exodus 13:21) so Jesus said, 'I am the light of the world. Whoever follows me will never walk in darkness, but will have the light of life' (John 8:12).

Just as the Nile was turned into blood so the water was turned into wine (John 2:1-11).

Just as Moses was a shepherd so Jesus is the good shepherd (John 10:11).

Just as Moses did miraculous signs so Jesus did miraculous signs (John 12:37).

Just as Moses parted the Red Sea so Jesus walked on the water (John 6:19).

Just as Moses received God's commandments on a mountain so Jesus expounded God's commandments on a mountainside (Matthew 5:1 – 8:1) and added a new commandment of his own (John 13:34).

Just as Moses was a prophet so was Jesus a prophet (Acts 3:22).

Just as Moses experienced health and healing so Jesus healed the sick (Exodus 15:26).

Just as Moses' face shone when he came down from Mount Sinai (Exodus 34:29-35) so Jesus was transfigured on a mountain in the presence of Moses and 'His face shone like the sun' (Matthew 17:2). Paul says the radiant glory from Christ is 'ever-increasing' while the one on Moses' face was 'fading away' (2 Corinthians 3:7-18).

Just as Moses had thirteen tribes of which one was a tribe of priests, so Jesus formed a band of thirteen with himself as the high priest (Hebrews 8).

Just as Moses sacrificed a lamb at Passover so Jesus, the lamb of God, was sacrificed at Passover (John 19:14).

'Just as Moses lifted up the snake in the desert, so the Son of Man must be lifted up, that everyone who believes in him may have eternal life' (John 3:14-15).

Just as Moses made an old covenant with God and said: 'This is the blood of the covenant, which God has commanded you to keep' (Hebrews 9:20), Christ by his blood is the 'mediator of a new covenant which promises an 'eternal inheritance' to those who believe (Hebrews 9:14-15).

'Just as Moses was faithful in all God's house Jesus has been found worthy of greater honour than Moses' (Hebrews 3:2-3).

PROPHECIES CONCERNING JESUS

The virgin will be with child and will give birth to a son, and will call him Immanuel (Isaiah 7:14).

He will honour Galilee of the Gentiles . . . For to us a child is born, to us a son is given, and the government will be on his shoulders. And he will be called Wonderful Counsellor, Mighty God, Everlasting Father, Prince of Peace. Of the increase of his government and peace there will be no end (Isaiah 9:1,6,7).

But you, Bethlehem Ephrathah, though you are small among the clans of Judah, out of you will come for me one who will be ruler over Israel, whose origins are from of old, from ancient times (Micah 5:2).

Nations will come to your light, and Kings to the brightness of your dawn . . . bearing gold and incense and proclaiming the praise of the Lord (Isaiah 60:3,6).

A shoot will come up from the stump of Jesse; from his roots a Branch will bear fruit. The Spirit of the Lord will rest on him – the Spirit of wisdom and of understanding, the Spirit of counsel and of power, the Spirit of knowledge and of the fear of the Lord (Isaiah 11:1-2).

The Spirit of the Lord is on me, because he has anointed me to preach good news to the poor. He has sent me to proclaim freedom for the prisoners and recovery of sight for the blind, to release the oppressed, to proclaim the year of the Lord's favour (Luke 4:18-19 based on Isaiah 61:1-2).

Rejoice greatly, O Daughter of Zion! Shout, Daughter of Jerusalem! See, your king comes to you, righteous and having salvation, gentle and riding on a donkey, on a colt, the foal of a donkey (Zechariah 9:9).

He was despised and rejected by men . . . surely he took up our infirmities and carried our sorrows. . . he was pierced for our transgressions, he was crushed for our iniquities; the punishment that brought us peace was upon him, and by his wounds we are healed . . . the Lord has laid on him the iniquity of us all . . . He was oppressed and afflicted, yet he did not open his mouth; he was led like a lamb to the slaughter, and as a sheep before her shearers is silent, so he did not open his mouth . . . He was assigned a grave with the wicked, and with the rich in his death . . . he bore the sin of many, and made intercession for the transgressors (Isaiah 53:3-12).

Dogs have surrounded me; a band of evil men has encircled me, they have pierced my hands and my feet. I can count all my bones; people stare and gloat over me. They divide my garments among them and cast lots for my clothing (Psalm 22:16-18).

'In that day,' declares the Sovereign Lord, 'I will make the sun go down at noon and darken the earth in broad daylight' (Amos 8:9).

Listen, O high priest Joshua and your associates seated before you, who are men symbolic of things to come: I am going to bring my servant, the Branch . . . and I will remove the sin of this land in a single day (Zechariah 3:8-9).

'The time is coming,' declares the Lord, 'when I will make a new covenant with the house of Israel and with the house of Judah . . . I will forgive their wickedness and will remember their sins no more' (Jeremiah 31:31-34).

Then will the eyes of the blind be opened and the ears of the deaf unstopped. Then will the lame leap like a deer, and the mute tongue shout for joy. Water will gush forth in the wilderness and streams in the desert (Isaiah 35:5-6).

He will baptise you with the Holy Spirit and with fire (Matthew 3:11).

BIBLE STUDY NOTES FOR LEADERS

Six is a good number to throw at the start of a game and also a good number to have for a discussion group. Once we go over twelve there will always be some who feel too inhibited to contribute. Throughout the book I have normally used the NIV version of the Bible unless otherwise stated. Any version will do but it may be easier if everyone has the same one. Some find it is better to play a professionally recorded tape of the appropriate passage rather than 'reading round' while others find a 'verse each' gets everyone speaking early on. Sensitivity, particularly to poorer readers, is crucial. It is always good to have a prayer at the start as we need God's help to understand his word, and it is also good to have a prayer at the end as we need God's help to obey his word.

Chapter One – In the Beginning

A trick question: Nothing.

Belief in the divinity of Jesus is a vital building-block in orthodox Christian belief. This chapter and this study seeks to establish that the Bible reveals Jesus as creator and God. His role in creation confirms his divinity and his divinity confirms his role in creation.

1. The New Testament says Jesus made the world and, of course, 'God' is also correct.
2. Jesus is God. (See Appendix 1). No one made Jesus. He

was in the beginning.

3. In John 3:19 sin and a love of evil are seen as the reasons why people do not recognise Jesus.

4. In John's Gospel the main reason given for the rejection of Jesus is his claim to be God. To an orthodox Jew this would be seen as blasphemy (John 10:30-33). Other answers such as jealousy, fear of the Romans (John 11:47-48) and the expectation of a political Messiah leading them into battle are also relevant (John 18:10).

5. The transfiguration of Jesus is not recorded in John but there are seven signs (see Chapter Two), a voice from heaven (John 12:28), his life, his love, his teaching, his death, his resurrection and his baptising in the Holy Spirit which reveal his glory (John 20:22).

6. All four Gospels suggest that Jesus laid aside his omnipotence, his omniscience and his omnipresence but not his holiness, nor righteousness, when he became flesh. (See Chapter Two).

7. We become children of God by believing and receiving Jesus. John 3:1-16 is also important and worth a look if there is time.

Chapter Two – Born Again of the Spirit

A silly question: No – not honey – John *the* Baptist, Attila *the* Hun and Winnie *the* Pooh all have the same middle name.

The problem with our secular and materialistic world is that many people live as though they are only flesh – until death comes home. Then they want a Christian funeral, to be told there is life after death and that the spirit of their loved one has gone to be with Jesus in heaven. In my opinion it would be more helpful if people could be encouraged to think about their 'spirit', made in the image of God, before they die.

1. Nicodemus believed Jesus performed miracles because God was with him. Jesus believed it was because he was

'in the Father' and the Father was in him (John 14:11).

2. We can see the kingdom of God by being 'born again' (John 3:3).

3. We can enter the kingdom of God by being born of water and Spirit. The 'water' is often debated. Some see it as our first normal human birth; some see it as baptism; some see it as being washed symbolically clean by the act of true repentance. Personally I prefer to take no chances and go for all three. Born of the Spirit with a capital 'S' is generally considered to mean receiving the Holy Spirit at conversion. Be born, repent, believe, be baptised in water, be baptised in the Holy Spirit, to my mind, = born again (See Acts 2:38).

4. Our spirits come alive when the Holy Spirit comes and resides in them. (See also Romans 8:9-11.)

5. Jesus is qualified to speak of heavenly things because he comes from heaven (John 3:12-13).

6. Jesus was lifted up on the cross (John 12:32).

7. We are born again, enter the kingdom of God, and receive eternal life when we repent of our sins, believe and trust in Jesus and receive him into our lives by his Holy Spirit (John 3:15, Romans 8:9-11). Baptism in water is the outward physical sign of all this and varies slightly in style according to the practice of different denominations.

Chapter Three – The Image of the Invisible God

An interesting question: Adam is 'the son of God', ie no human parents (Luke 3:38).

My own experience suggests to me that many people do not come to church and do not become Christians because they are afraid of the God of love. I believe one of our aims as Christians should be to help people meet the God of love in Jesus.

1. The disciples knew what God the Father was like because they saw him in Jesus.

2. They got to know God the Father because they got to know Jesus.
3. They entered heaven and the presence of Father God by believing and trusting in Jesus.
4. The miraculous signs helped the disciples to believe in Jesus especially when he turned water into wine. Our own sin, sin done to us, bad modelling of a father and poor, non-biblical teaching can distort the image of God within us.
5. We can know what God the Father is like by reading about Jesus in the Gospels.
6. We can know God the Father through the Holy Spirit who indwells all who believe in Jesus. We can go to heaven when we die by believing and trusting in Jesus now.
7. We can help others to believe in God by praying (John 14:13-14) and by doing what Jesus did through faith in him (John 14:12). If there is time, people in the group might like to make some further suggestions as well.

Chapter Four – The Church

A teasing question: Enoch (Genesis 5:24) and Elijah never died (2 Kings 2:11), Jesus never lied (1 Peter 2:22), and Methuselah, the son of Enoch, was the oldest man who ever lived (Genesis 5:21-27).

Jesus praying for the Church, which will become his body here on earth after his ascension into heaven, is a wonderful illustration of how Christians can continue Jesus' work and presence after his departure and before his return. Many people today try to say 'yes' to Jesus and 'no' to the Church but that was not a possibility Jesus ever considered. To become a Christian is to become a member of the body of Christ with obligations.

1. Jesus is praying for the Church.
2. The world will believe when Christians are one with God

the Father, one with God the Son, one with God the Holy Spirit and one with each other.

3. The world will know that God loves Jesus and the Church when we love God the Holy Trinity and the body of Christ.

4. When we love God and one another in total unity then Jesus' prayers will be answered. I suspect most of us still have some distance to travel on this and need help from the Holy Spirit.

5. Jesus wants us to see his glory in heaven and to share it with him.

6. Loving God, loving one another and making Jesus known are the most important things in Church life, according to this prayer of Jesus.

7. The Holy Spirit in us helps us to know Jesus and to make him known.

Chapter Five – All One in Christ

A daily question:- Today.

Notice that Jesus put himself in a vulnerable place by speaking to a Samaritan woman with a bad reputation, but *no apartheid* was not his only aim. Jesus used it as a bridge to bring home the gospel.

1. As an eye-witness John may just have been using the land owned by Jacob and Joseph to identify the exact spot or he may have been pointing out to his readers that Jews and Samaritans come from the same ancestors, share the same land and worship the same God.

2. In John's day the 'Gnostics' did not believe that Jesus really came in the flesh. Being 'tired' emphasises Jesus' true humanity and suggests that an eye-witness recorded the story.

3. The passage informs us that the Samaritan woman was surprised because Jews did not normally speak to Samaritans. I think the male/female, respectable/outcast

relationship would also have surprised people at the time. There is no biblical evidence to suggest that Jesus received a drink.

4. Jesus was saying he loves everyone equally and 'without prejudice'. It is all too easy to become prejudiced against people of different nationalities. A recent survey suggested 90% of people in Britain were racist. Culture, sex and class can also divide us. Listening to one another and to God is always helpful.

5. Jesus can help us. The 'living water' he offers is the Holy Spirit.

6. Jesus gives the Holy Spirit to those who ask. See also Luke 11:13.

7. The comparison between Jesus as 'God' and Jacob as 'man' is beyond classification but the comparison between Jesus as 'man' and Jacob as 'man' is worth noting. There are too many differences to list here but do notice how frequently Jacob was economical with the truth.

Chapter Six – Signs and Wonders

A topical question: We can look at life through heaven's eyes by going to see the Spielberg film, *Prince of Egypt*, (the words are taken from one of its songs), or by reading the Bible, or by asking God to fill us with his Holy Spirit. I'm keen on all three.

In our 'Post-Modern' society people are not as convinced by words or arguments as experience, but the great news is that Jesus has not left us comfortless. We have some great 'words' in the Bible, many, many good reasons to believe, and the presence of the Holy Spirit to confirm the 'words' from God to us in experience. We really can 'know' God as well as 'know about him', as Jeremiah prophesied.

1. Jesus' disciples believed in him because of the miracles he did.

2. People believed what Jesus' disciples said because of the signs and wonders they did in Jesus' name.

3. The greater things Jesus will do through us by his Spirit are: more teaching, more belief, more believers, more righteousness, more pastoral care, more truth, more power and more blessings. In other words more of the same because the Holy Spirit is in more people. Those filled with the Holy Spirit can do these things. Faith in Jesus means doing what he says, in the Bible, and by his Spirit.

4. We can only ask Jesus to do things with which he agrees. This is what 'in my name' means. Faith in Christ and obedience to Christ are always closely related.

5. Jesus and the Father, who are one, send the Holy Spirit.

6. Jesus always refers to the Holy Spirit as 'he' and never 'it'.

7. We are filled with the Holy Spirit, the first time, by becoming Christians. We are continually filled after that by continually asking God to fill us.

Chapter Seven – True Worshippers

A theological question: Some would say it was Jesus – a possible Christophany number five.

It is very difficult trying to help people to worship in spirit by discussing words. The experience on the inside when people are filled afresh with the Holy Spirit is one of moving from singing songs to worshipping the living God, but the words can sometimes help people to seek for something more, and that is the aim of this study.

1. The woman's response indicates that Jesus knew what sins she had committed because the Spirit revealed them to him. She recognised Jesus as a prophet – a person who received information in a supernatural, rather than a natural, way.

2. One suspects from the rest of the story that Jesus saw the

encounter as an opportunity to share the good news about himself with some Samaritans.

3. Everyone is welcome to come to the body of Christ and hear the gospel, as the woman at the well did, but those who wish to belong are expected to respond to sin, as God defines it, like David did. Confession and repentance are necessary if we are to become true worshippers, but pastoral sensitivity and love are also needed if we are to help others to become true worshippers.

4. Jesus implies that worship 'in spirit and in truth' no longer depends on any specific location but moves the activity into the unseen, spiritual realm.

5. We become equipped as true worshippers, according to John, by believing in Jesus who is truth (John 14:6), and . . .

6. receiving the Holy Spirit so that our spirits come alive (John 3:6).

7. Once equipped we need to choose to worship God, wherever we are, as an act of our will.

Chapter Eight – Prophecy

A powerful question: God.

Our God is a God who speaks. He loves to be known by his children. He lives inside every born-again believer but many do not know that and many do not expect him to speak. It is my experience that when Christians expect God to speak they hear him.

1. When something painful happens it is often easier for believers to accept it when it has been prophesied in Scripture beforehand.

2. Jesus prophesies about Judas so they will still believe in Jesus' divinity when betrayal takes place. A fulfilled prophecy is always encouraging even when it hurts.

3. Like the story of Hosea and the Northern Kingdom it may not be too late for Judas to repent; or, like Peter,

after he has let Jesus down, he could be encouraged by the 'word' to come back and be forgiven. Supremely it reveals the love of Jesus.

4. 'Night' is used to emphasise the darkness of the deed. Our discoveries about David, Manasseh and Peter earlier in the book would suggest that Judas, too, could have been forgiven if he had repented.

5. There are eleven commandments in the Bible and the eleventh is the hardest. To love as Jesus loved, in my opinion, is harder than anything else.

6. After Jesus' death, remembrance of the prophecy may have brought some comfort and encouraged belief. Thomas seemed to find 'figures of speech' difficult (John 16:29).

7. I think Jesus predicted Peter's denial so that when it happened Peter wouldn't run away, knowing Jesus knew and still loved him. The New Testament suggests all Christians can prophesy from time to time (Acts 2:18; 1 Corinthians 14:31,39). Confirmed words, which we can then claim to be from God, often encourage us and help us to obey him.

Chapter Nine – The Cost of Discipleship

A thoughtful question: The answer is to be found in Matthew 10:39. The key is Jesus. Whoever gives his life to Jesus will live, even though he dies, in heaven for ever.

This was a saying the missionary Jim Elliott quoted frequently, prior to taking the gospel of Christ to the Auca Indians in the Ecuador jungle. It was there he became a Christian martyr at the end of a spear. Afterwards some of the tribe who murdered him became Christians.

Nothing demonstrates spiritual warfare more clearly than the persecution of Jesus and his followers. Despite living for truth, justice and love, the world opposes them and sometimes kills them. 'Then the dragon was enraged at the woman

and went off to make war against the rest of her offspring –
those who obey God's commandments and hold to the testimony of Jesus' (Revelation 12:17).

Although the gospel of Jesus Christ is very good news we
also have a solemn duty to share the cost of discipleship.

1. The world opposes God the Father, Jesus and Christians
    because of sin and because they have never known God
    the Father or God the Son.

2. We can help people to know Jesus by testifying to him,
    his claims, and the difference he can make in our lives.

3. The Holy Spirit helps us to testify about Jesus. (See also
    Matthew 10:19-20.)

4. Those who follow Jesus are likely to be treated in the
    same way as Jesus was treated.

5. Persecution varies according to culture, climate and conti-
    nent. In Birmingham we found people of other faiths
    could be violent towards us. We were stoned, flooded and
    our trees set on fire. Often, however, it may just be
    ridicule, loss of status or occasionally loss of job, at pre-
    sent, in the British Isles.

6. Jesus warned us beforehand about persecution so that we
    would not lose our faith when it happened but realise that
    Jesus was right again.

7. The early Church was 'highly regarded by the people' but
    also persecuted (Acts 5:13,17-18). It is not easy to make
    rules, but obviously if no one at work knows we are
    Christians we will not be mocked for our faith. Wearing
    crosses or fish-badges round our necks or in our lapels
    should soon put that right.

Chapter Ten – The Cross

An important question: 'There is now no condemnation for
those who are in Christ Jesus' (Romans 8:1). Those who are
in Christ escape the judgement and are accepted by God.
Praying a prayer of commitment to Christ, meaning it and

living as though we mean it is being in Christ. Getting on the first step of the escalator ensures we get to the top and avoid the judgement because by doing so we place ourselves in the hands of our merciful God.

Some church people don't tell others about Jesus because they are not sure where they stand with him themselves. Try and use this look at the cross to help everyone present to be sure of salvation in Christ, and leave enough time for question seven. That may help us to evangelise more effectively.

1. John records that the proclamation of Christ as king was written in the three major languages of the civilised world so that all may see and understand. Noah's rainbow was good news for the whole world; so is the cross of Christ.

2. Calvary is thought by some to be on Mount Moriah. God sacrificed his son where Abraham's son Isaac received a reprieve.

3. Jesus was killed on the day of Preparation (John 19:31). Hyssop dipped in wine vinegar was offered to Jesus (John 19:29). Blood flowed out of Jesus' side on the cross like blood on the doorposts (John 19:34). Jesus drank the wine and said, 'It is finished' (John 19:30). See also John 6:53-59 where the Passover symbolism is taken even further. John is keen for his readers to understand that Jesus is the lamb of God who sets believers free from bondage and death spiritually, just as the blood of the lamb at the Exodus was used by God to set the people free physically.

4. There is a suspicion in this passage that Pilate was beginning to believe in the kingship of Jesus. Maybe, 'What I have written, I have written,' was the dramatic climax of the Roman governor coming to belief? Possibly. As King of the Jews, as King of kings, Jesus the Son of David extends the Davidic reign to all eternity.

5. John sees at least four Old Testament prophecies fulfilled at the cross and he doesn't even mention Isaiah 53.

6. It is strange that John doesn't mention the Father here. Luke has, 'Father, into your hands I commit my spirit'

and 'paradise' as Jesus' destination (Luke 23:43-56).

7. All spirits of people return to God at death, and those who believe and trust in Jesus go on to paradise.

Chapter Eleven – A New Creation

A subtle question: Lazarus came back from death, Jesus went through it; resuscitation rather then resurrection; Jesus went through the grave-clothes and left them behind but Lazarus came back from the tomb still bound; poor Lazarus would have to die again but not Jesus. Notice how Jesus' body is still recognisable – but only just – yet not so limited.

It is possible to use Christian belief to try and escape from the pain and to avoid facing reality and the responsibilities of living for Jesus here on earth. The Christian way, the Jesus way, is to face the pain of Gethsemane and Calvary and come through it to resurrection. If we seek to escape the pain of our own sins and the sin done to us by running away, our sin is ever before us, but if we face it with Jesus and come through it with him we put it behind us. This is the path to Christian healing and becoming new creations, but notice how Jesus does it sensitively with love.

1. Almost certainly this is the moment when Jesus restores Peter after he'd denied Jesus three times.

2. Peter was hurt for two reasons. 1) Three times Jesus seemed to question Peter's love for him. 2) Three times Jesus reminded him of his denial.

3. Jesus didn't hurt Peter but like a good counsellor reflected back to Peter the truth of his own sin which caused the pain. He did it out of love to heal him and restore him.

4. 'Feed my lambs' (John 21:15), 'Take care of my sheep' (John 21:16), and 'Feed my sheep' (John 21:17) reinstates Peter. He is still the shepherd of the flock, the leader, as declared publicly by Jesus in front of *seven* apostles.

5. Doubting Thomas is present. Jesus had come to him in front of the other disciples, helped him to face the pain of his own doubt and to come through it to glorious belief. Showing Thomas his hands and side was like asking Peter three times if he loved him.

6. Peter is the pastor but not the king. We are all called to feed one another and care for one another but not to dominate one another or be jealous of one another. (See Appendix 2.)

7. Jesus helped Peter to face his pain – the pain of his own sin – but he also helped him to be forgiven and to feel forgiven. I believe Jesus wants to do the same for all of us.